BECOME AN UNSTOPPABLE STORYTELLER

How to Craft Compelling Serials

2nd Edition

KIMBOO YORK

House of York

This book is dedicated to Gina Hogan Edwards, writer and editor extraordinaire, who held my hand through the speed run of getting this book together and published. Thank you for your willing support, your kind ear, and your excellent feedback! This would not have happened without you.

Preface for the Print Edition

Earlier printed copies of this book did not include any way to find the online resources I mention in the text. This was a major oversight on my part, and I apologize!

I have created a webpage with links to every online site/resource for you. If you have any issues with the links, please email me at kimboo@houseofyork.info.

RESOURCES LINK:

https://houseofyork.info/serials-links/

Contents

Introduction

EVERYTHING OLD IS NEW AGAIN

Serial stories are everything old and new about storytelling, and in ~~2023~~ 2026 they're entering a renaissance.

The dawn of storytelling in human history was quite possibly born out of serialized stories. Consider the old, beloved conceit of *One Thousand and One Nights*, where Scheherazade staves off her own execution by spinning an endless story that she leaves on a cliffhanger every night. She spun an endless, unstoppable story… in short, she told a serialized tale that eventually saved her life.

In truth, *One Thousand and One Nights* is a collection of much older tales, some assumed to go back thousands of years. They are merely bound together by the pretense of Scheherazade's life in the balance, but clearly the idea that a person could use "continual storytelling" to hold an audience captive is an ancient one.

Many cultures have folklore about the traveling bards or storytellers who showed up in the village to spin a story that lasted for days or weeks in exchange for sustenance and/or money. In China, the ancient tradition of quyi is the art of storytelling and is represented by the lone narrator spinning a story on a street corner or in a tea shop, often ongoing for weeks (even months) as more of the story is revealed every day.

In the West, most epic stories and poems that were eventually preserved in writing (the *Epic of Gilgamesh*, the *Odyssey*, and later *Beowulf*) first lived for centuries as oral narratives shared in serialized form over multiple tellings. That is not even counting the oral traditions that resulted in ancient religious scriptures from around the world, such as the Hebrew Bible, the Vedas, and the Mahabharata.

Thanks to the movable type revolution, the printed book slowly took over as the primary transmission for literature in the 16th century, and it became common for a "story" to be a self-contained product with a beginning, a middle, and an end. In short: a novel. In this book, I take pains to differentiate "novel" from "serial," because I consider them to be two different forms, and between the two, novels are the newcomers.

Exceptions abound and academics argue over specific dates and formats, but in general, the novel as we know it now is relatively recent. The very first acknowledged modern *novel* in human history is *The Tale of Genji* by Murasaki Shikibu, which appeared on- scene only as late as the 11th century (conjecture, as the actual date of creation is unknown, but if anything, is earlier than that). In the Western tradition, Roman proto-novels existed as early as the 1st century b.c.e.! But novels *modern* readers would recognize as such (that is, prose stories in book form) did not appear until roughly the 15th century.

One thousand years might look like a long time, but consider for a moment that writing has been around for at *least* 6,000 years, and recognizable spoken language between 100,000 and 200,000 years.

However, even with the rise of The Novel as an Art Form (capitalization added for pretentiousness), serials persisted. The most common example cited these days is Charles Dickens, who was paid by the word to write ongoing stories for magazines. Throughout the 20th century, serialized stories appeared in magazines of all types until they started waning in popularity in the 1960s. Novel series, such as the classic Kinsey Millhone series by Sue Grafton, stepped in to fill the demand for serials. People have always wanted ongoing stories with primary and recurring characters, and the publishing industry did its best to meet that demand based on the printing and distribution technologies they had at the time.

Nowadays, serials are on the cusp of becoming a major force for storytelling in the West. *Everything old is new again!*

In some parts of the world, though, serials had *already* become a cultural phenomenon long before I got a clue.

My eyes were opened when I landed in Chinese drama fandom in 2020. I was vaguely aware then that webnovels existed, and I knew about long-running, serialized mangas out of Japan. I had also come across a few independently minded authors who were serializing their books on personal websites or Patreon. Other platforms appeared and becoming more popular, too. As a fanfiction reader, I was (very!) familiar with the "chaptered" (serialized) stories on the fanfiction repository Archive of Our Own (AO3). Wattpad was founded in 2007, but it took a few years before it got its claws into young readers and writers of romance (and fanfiction) to become the powerhouse it is now. Radish hit in 2017 and quickly gained a solid foothold, at least for a while (more about why it died in 2025 later, when I discuss platforms).

So, yes, I knew *serialized stories* were out there and were popular, but even as the numbers skyrocketed, they were a very small piece of the publishing pie. Serialized online novels were the outliers.

All of that paled in comparison to what I discovered about the Chinese webnovel industry.

Stories on webnovel platforms such as JJWXC and Qidian get *billions* of reads and are often hundreds of thousands of words long. Some top over 1 million words in length. (Note: "word count" here is approximate, since the original works are in written Chinese, which use characters that are logosyllabic. Thus, these numbers are based on the English translations. Point being: very, *very* long stories!)

The West is finally catching up, though, and serialized stories (novels and serials) are undergoing a renaissance because of the internet and changing technology (I talk about current examples in the chapter <u>Serials in Practice</u>). Ten years ago, it was difficult to serialize a story online in the West; outside of fanfiction sites, Wattpad and Patreon were the only two services that made it easy, and one of them only allowed you to post without charging the reader (Patreon did not allow free tiers until 2023; you could "follow" a creator but they had no way to incentivize people to do so). While you could build your own website (and some did) to have paid subscriptions to your stories, it required time, money, and knowledge (or *more* money) to DIY it.

But times they are a'changin'! Ream launched in May 2023. (*Disclaimer*: I was one of the beta authors for the platform, and I'll be talking more about why that was important for me in the next chapter.) Other platforms, such as Substack, RoyalRoad, Medium, and more, are making story serializations and subscriptions for authors possible. Webhosting platforms like Wix and Squarespace, and even Shopify have implemented "membership" features that allow authors to create their own private communities of fans. Authors are using WordPress plugins or sales platforms like Gumroad and FourthWall to serialize their work. Patreon has been the home base for many authors for well over a decade.

The changing face of technology (obligatory reference to "artificial intelligence," yada yada yada) has led to the rise of what is now called the *creator economy*.

No, you don't need to write million-word epics in order to have a subscription author platform, but the option is there. On the other hand, having a subscription platform of your own means that you can write until a story is *finished*, however long that takes, instead of writing to a word count or an end beat (not that there's anything wrong with that!). As I explain later in this book, novels are a discrete form of storytelling that have their own traditional structures, and "the novel" has risen to become a respected art form, but it is not the *only* way to tell a long story. Serials are different and can be built in a variety of ways so you can continue telling your story with the goal of keeping readers addicted for however long you want.

If that appeals to you, then welcome to the world of serials, where unstoppable stories live!

My Serials Story

In 2017, I published my *very big book*, Wolves of Harmony Heights. It started as a NaNoWriMo (National Novel Writing Month) lark in 2015 and ended up in 2017 at 200,000 words of witches, werewolves, and a polyamorous MMF (male-male-female) romance.

It kept getting longer and longer as I wrote it, and my friend and story advisor Kim kept telling me to chop it in half or into thirds. She thought I could package it as a tril-ogy, which after all is a popular form of book content.

I couldn't.

There was no natural break at the halfway point or at any third. I would have had to rewrite it significantly—move scenes around, change character arcs, etc.—to fit the conventions of "novels tied together as a trilogy." I was stymied by that, even as I understood the problem.

What I did not understand was the *cause* of the problem:

I failed to account for my fanfiction habit.

By 2017, I had been writing serialized stories for ten years *in the form of fanfiction*. My most popular fanfic are multi-chaptered stories usually written on the fly and posted as I wrote them. They were often more compact stories than true-blue epic serials, but when I reread them now, it is clear I was writing each chapter to be consumed as part of a serial, not as chapters of a novel.

I was caught in a feedback loop of enjoying writing fanfic that way, which led inevitably to the unintended consequence of *training* my mind to write that way.

The result was that as I wrote *Wolves of Harmony Heights*, I was unintentionally *writing it as a serial*. I wrote it to be read in bite-sized chapters over a long period of time, and I honestly had no idea why it just seemed to keep going... and going...

Self-awareness: zero.

I was tangentially aware of epic, long-running serials, but at the time, I was fully immersed in the self-publishing community as an author trying to find her way to success. All the advice for authors was geared toward writing and selling *novels in the form of books*, which made total sense, since in the Western world books reign supreme (and, admittedly, still do). You published books to be sold in a bookstore (online or not); what could be more obvious than that?

The result was that I felt pulled in several directions. I was deeply committed to the mindset that "original stories are *novels* you sell as *books,*" yet I was (unintentionally) writing a *serial* that, by its very nature, was going to be an outlier of a book.

In the (literal) end, even at 200k words, the book has a rushed ending. Fortunately, none of the novel's (very few) readers ever complained about it, but to this day, I keep toying with the idea of serializing it and re-writing the ending. I probably won't, but the temptation is there because now I know full well that it is, and *was always meant to be*, a *serial*.

But how did I figure that out?

I had already toyed with the idea of serialization in 2018 with the original concept for my story *Dragon's Grail*, which I planned to make a series of novellas. I imagined a story consisting of ten 30,000-word novellas, so 300,000 words in all. I was excited! Then I wrote the first novella and the whole thing fell apart. I did write the next two novellas in the series and drafted two more, but I was having the same old problem I'd had with my earlier works: trying to write to market, write/publish fast, and advertise for readers.

Most authors are not keen on marketing, so I just assumed I was guilty as charged. *Marketing! Ugh! What a pain, amirite?!?!?!*

Turns out, I was definitely not keen on marketing, but the problem was not *me*. The problem was my entire approach to my career as an author.

It would be a lie to say I never wanted to hit the best-seller lists, but on the whole, my goal was never to *just* write popular books. I wanted more out of being an author than targeting my niche and writing to market to rake in a lot of money.

Honestly? All I've ever wanted to do was to write the stories I have in my heart, waiting to be told, to readers who want to read them.

The failure of *Dragon's Grail* was on a continuum along with my frustrations over *Wolves of Harmony Heights* and my enjoyment of writing fanfiction: *I was a serials author living in a novel-focused world.*

I looked at people writing original fiction on Wattpad and I was so damn envious. Yet I held myself back because, gosh, what was my *niche*? What was my novel-writing goal? Who was my super-specific demographic?

I did not have answers to those questions.

As I mentioned, I got involved with several Chinese drama fandoms in late 2019 and early 2020, which was great timing as they carried me emotionally through the pandemic lock-down. My dramas of choice (*Guardian*; *The Untamed*, based on *The Grandmaster of Demonic Cultivation*; and *Nirvana in Fire*), all started out as webnovels, and having read them in translations, I categorize *Nirvana in Fire* as an actual novel but the other two are definitely serials. (If you are not sure of the difference, check out the glossary, or skip forward to the *Serials are Different* section!)

Through those fandoms, I discovered other webnovels (notably, *Heaven Official's Blessing*), which were incredibly long and complex and absolutely enthralling stories.

While I am, by academic training, a student of the history of text technologies (sometimes called 'the history of the book'), my focus has always been on the development of text in Western European history. I am not well-versed on the storytelling traditions that manga and Chinese webnovels are built on, so I can only give you the personal impression I had at the time I discovered stories like *Grandmaster of Demonic Cultivation*, *Guardian*, and *Heaven Official's Blessing*: **I want to do that**.

I want to tell *unstoppable* stories that become epic tales that readers crave. I want to explore the lives of the characters I obsess over. I want to share my joy and amazement with readers in a way that draws them in and never, ever, lets go.

I've been a part of enough fandoms to know what it means to love a story that much, from *Star Wars: A New Hope* (1977) down the decades to *The Untamed* (2019), and all the fanfiction in between. You have too, I imagine.

I knew what I *wanted*, but I did not know what I was looking at.

MY SEARCH FOR A CONCEPT

Fast-forward to 2019: after suffering through self-publishing *Wolves of Harmony Heights* (to a *very* limited audience), I realized my instinct to write "sprawling epics" was something I needed to stop fighting.

It was because I had not yet fully realized that **a serial is a distinct story form** (more on that later) that I originally conceived *Dragon's Grail* as a novella series that I would publish serially.

In other words, I was thinking in the traditional terms of *a book series as a collection of novels/novellas*.

To that end, I worked up a (very) basic spreadsheet on writing a series and shared it with a few author friends in a writers' forum for feedback. One said something along the lines of, "Think of writing a novel series like writing a television show, where each book is an episode, and all the books together are a full season." That advice is repeated today by a lot of people, but when I heard it in 2019, it was still fresh.

That was my "a-ha!" moment. I finally saw *that writing a serial is distinct from writing a novel*.

But what did that mean in practice? What is a serial, and how is one structured?

In addition to examining classics I was familiar with— *Dune* (novel), *Chronicles of Narnia* (serial), *The Hobbit* (novel), *The Lord of the Rings* (serial), and of course *Great Expectations* (serial)—I took a closer look at the Chinese dramas I was watching and, from there, the webnovels they were based on.

While the mindbogglingly massive popularity of webnovels in Asian countries truly opened my eyes to the potential of serialized *serial* storytelling, I was still having problems identifying the elements that make a serial, other than the common description of "very, very long."

Then I picked up the book *Save the Cat: The Last Book on Screenwriting You'll Ever Need*, by Blake Snyder, and everything changed.

Snyder released his concept into the world in 2005, and for a few years, it was passed around mostly by script writers as a holy grail before gaining traction with indie authors. A lot of authors have come across Save the Cat!™ story beats second hand, and so are unaware (or forget) that it is an outline for *motion pictures*, but there is no denying that it is a great recipe for good storytelling. It has been adapted for novels and television, and many, many authors swear by it.

I was a real late-comer, picking it up in 2020!

The exact moment when I conceptualized what makes a serial structure different from a novel was when I finally understood what he meant by "Break into Two" and "Break into Three." Those are what he calls his bridging beats, the moment when one act "breaks" into the next one. In movies, these are critical moments when you can lose the audience completely. They will leave to go buy popcorn or secretly check their phone (or make out? I forget what we did before smartphones, tbh) or worse, just stop caring. Every Save the Cat!™ beat is meant to keep the audience engaged, but the "break" beats are critical.

I looked at the Chinese novels-actually-serials I was reading (translations, mind you), as well as the long-running novel series I loved and a few recent English-language hit serials on RoyalRoad, and it finally came to me: **whichever structure a serial uses, it has to use *more than one*, and it has to do so in a way that is continually self-generating.**

(Don't worry, I explain that concept in the next chapter!)

WHAT IS THIS BOOK ABOUT?

The goal of this book is to help you look at serials as another tool in your authorial arsenal. Some of the most popular, addictive stories in the history of the world are serials—among them, the *Iliad*, *Lord of the Rings*, *Star Wars*, *Berserk*, and *Grandmaster of Demonic Cultivation*—which inspire incredible reader loyalty and create lifelong superfans. It is an amazing art form!

When writing this book, I made the general assumption that you, dear reader, are a writer already familiar with the basics, such as story structure and narrative, and other jargon. If you've never in your life heard the phrase "three-act story structure," then you might get lost quickly!

However, you don't have to be a published author or even a writer who has ever finished a story (yet!) to get some value from the ideas herein. My goal is to provide you with tools you can use to create addictive stories, no matter where you are on your authorial journey.

I've broken this up into two main sections, which you can read in order or out of order (or skip parts if you want). This is not an academic treatise after all. It is meant to be used as a tool kit: grab what you want to use next, as needed.

The next section, Basics of Serials, goes deep into *what* a serial story is, why you might want to embrace the form as an author, and different ways to approach it. First, there is more about the *exciting history of books* (exciting! I swear!!!) as I explain what makes serials different from other story forms. Then I give you an in-depth look at the benefits of serials for both authors and readers and explain why the serial is such a great format for authors looking to expand (or start) an online subscription service for their writing. The sections comparing serials to 'novel series' are important to read if you are thinking about turning a book series into a serial *or* if you eventually want to publish your serial as a collection of printed books. Finally, I define the different types of serial styles, since picking a serial style is a great way to help you decide which story beats structure will work best for your story.

If you'd rather just jump to the action, though, head over to the chapter Serial Beats. The Overview section is an excellent cheat sheet of everything that follows, but you can also just keep reading past that to get a full in-depth explanation of the serial beats structure I have created. I break down the way story structure beats can be used in your stories to make them *unstoppable stories,* by which I mean stories you want to keep writing and stories readers want to keep reading!

Finally, I provide some examples of how you can set up your serial for maximum distribution. There many ways to deliver episodes (individual installments of the story) to your readers, and you don't have to use an online subscription platform to do it (although I recommend that, for many reasons!).

If you enjoy making stories that are rich tapestries of narrative story arcs *and* you are willing to invest into long-term world-building, then you (yes you!) might just be a serials author!

Glossary

I am providing this for you, the reader's, convenience, but I assure you it was originally created in order to keep me from making a mess of things!

While glossaries are usually placed at the end of a book, gaining a meaningful grasp on the concepts presented here relies on a shared understanding of the terminology. So I've chosen to put it upfront. Don't worry, though, there will not be a test at the end!

This glossary became necessary when *I started confusing myself* with the terms everyone throws around. I have a Master's degree in Library and Information Studies with a concentration in the History of Text Technologies (a.k.a. "History of the Book), but even so, I was getting myself twisted up using some terms when I actually meant something else.

Disclaimer: I'm not claiming these are all dictionary-perfect definitions of these words. This glossary explains how *I* am using these terms in *this* book. Some terms I've created from whole cloth, while others are interpretations

I've made for the sake of clarity. Please do not sic the OED on me!

Au courant writing: Writing a story and publishing/posting parts of it before it is complete.

Beats: Story beats are the smallest units of storytelling that collectively build scenes, sequences, acts, and the overall narrative. They are key moments or events that propel the plot forward. Like individual notes in a song, beats give a story its rhythm, shaping its pace and direction. These can involve character actions, decisions, conflicts, or revelations. In outlining a story, beats ensure consistent pacing, character development, and plot progression.

Book: A compendium or collection of information which can comprise either fiction or non-fiction in the shape of a product that can be shared or sold in physical or digital format. Historically, books are found in a wide variety of formats, including scrolls and codices (singular: codex, which is what we think of as a book: sheets of paper between two covers), whether hand-written or printed, and these days includes audio books and ebooks. The term "book" is often used interchangeably with "novel," but it is actually distinct from it. Traditionally, all novels are books, but not all books are novels.

Chapter: Story segments resulting from the author's division of the narrative, plot, and character arcs in a way that clarifies and enhances the story. Chapters are common in novels; in serials, chapters sometimes equate to the beats of a story. (Also see *beats*)

Episode: A term taken from television production, where an episode is one installment of a longer run (season) of a show, but this is not a 1:1 analogy. While a single television episode has a whole story arc on its own, that can be broken down by beats, in serials *an episode is an installment of the story posted for reader consumption that at most represents a single beat of the story arc or just part of a single beat.* A serial episode often consists of just one scene, beat, or chapter.

Form: The general shape of a story, no matter the published format or internal structure. Examples include novels, novellas, serials, epic poems, and short stories.

Format: The physical or digital shape of a story product. Modern examples include printed books, ebooks, audiobooks, book series, and webnovels. Older examples include scrolls and clay tablets.

Installment: A single serial update consisting of just one scene, beat, or chapter. (See also *episode*)

Long Arc: In reference to serial beats as explained in this book, a long arc is the "long" narrative arc that extends over multiple seasons. A serial might have only one overarching long arc, or it might have several that overlap as the story progresses. (Also see *Beats* and *Seasons*)

Novel: A type of story form, usually comprising over 50,000 words of *fictional* prose depicting characters and action. A novel is a self-contained story most commonly found in the format of a book, but can also be published serially.

Novella: A type of story form, usually under 50,000 words of fictional prose depicting characters and action, most commonly found in the form of a self-contained, completed book.

Scene: A discrete part of an episode/chapter, often used to mark the passage of time, or a change in location or point of view.

Season: A term taken from television production, where a season is a set of 8 to 25 episodes (rarely more) aired during a specific timeframe. In the context of serials, a season is a series of beats/chapters that fully play out a story structure (e.g., three-act structure, Save the Cat!™, etc.).

Serial: A type of story form, usually over 100,000 words, designed to be shared sequentially in installments (chapters or scenes; i.e., episodes) over a period of time and containing overlapping story arcs. Although the serial is one of the oldest forms of storytelling, *it is a generative, dynamic form.* Serials are most familiar to people today as television shows.

Serialization: The delivery of a story to a reading audience sequentially in parts (chapters or installments; i.e., episodes). Any long story form or anthology can be serialized, but it is important to note that the act of chopping up a novel does not mean it is a "serial," only that it is being delivered in a serialized fashion. (Also see *Serial*)

Series: A meta-format for a group of books linked by a major story arc, a theme, or a cast of characters (or all of the above). Series are particularly popular in genres such as cozy mysteries, romance, action-adventure, and fantasy.

Series Void: A characteristic of long-running novel series when the repetition of the story structure becomes stale and readership falls off.

Short Arc (ShArc): In serials, a type of subplot (see *Subplot*) of a short duration with the main purpose of carrying reader interest over breaks or lulls in the story (e.g., between one season and another). ShArcs can be about side characters, feature a side quest to the main storyline, introduce new characters, or any number of options. Note that all ShArcs are subplots, but not all subplots are ShArcs.

Story: A narrative account of an event or a sequence of events, either true or fictitious, in prose or verse, which is crafted to entertain, inform, or inspire. One way of thinking about it is that *story = content*.

Story Arc: The path or progression of a storyline and its characters from the beginning of the story to the end. Story arc can be thought of as the "shape" of the story, and it often follows a pattern of rising and falling action. A story can have one overall arc, but it can also have smaller arcs within it. For example, a novel might have an overall story arc, but each chapter might have its own smaller arc. (Also see *Long Arc, Short Arc*)

Story Form: *see* Form

Structure: The way a story is arranged, usually identified by acts and beats. Popular story structures include the three-act story structure, the five-act story structure, the hero's journey, romancing the beats, and Save the Cat!™.

Subplot: A secondary plot or a minor/side story, or story thread that is subordinate to the main plot. Subplots often involve supporting characters, those besides the protagonist or antagonist. Subplots enrich a story by providing depth to characters, offering alternative perspectives, creating tension, and maintaining reader interest. They can also be used to flesh out a world or setting and to reveal aspects of the main characters.

ONE

Basics of Serials

SERIALS ARE DIFFERENT

This book is not about writing a novel you post sequentially as a "serialized novel."

This book is about creating *serial fiction*, a.k.a. ***unstoppable stories***.

To start with, I put a firm dividing line between "novel" and "serial," even though they overlap a lot in application. As I spell out in the Glossary:

- *Serial:* A type of story form, usually over 100,000 words, designed to be shared sequentially in installments (chapters or installments; i.e., episodes) over a period of time and contains overlapping story arcs. Although the serial is one of the oldest forms of storytelling, it is a generative, dynamic form. Serials are most familiar to people today as television shows.

- *Novel:* A type of story form, usually comprising over 50,000 words of fictional prose depicting characters and action. A novel is a self-contained story and is most commonly found in the format of a book, but can also be published serially.

A serial can become a book, and a novel might be a serialized story. In fact, many popular serialized fiction stories have been published as novels (although usually as a *series* of novels, as most serialized stories are too long to be reasonably and affordably published as a single book; more on that in Serial vs. Series).

The common perception is that the difference between a serial and a novel is simply the *delivery method*: novels are published as individual products, and serials are published in installments until they are completed, at which point they are re-packaged as a novel.

Sure, you could decide to just write a novel, publish its chapters serially, and call that a "serial." No one would stop you and honestly, no one would complain! Many subscription-based authors exclusively publish serialized novels, and are happy doing so, and so are their readers, and no one cares what they call them.

However, if you want to create *unstoppable stories*, it will help to change your mindset to consider novels and serials as two fundamentally different forms of storytelling. They share a lot of features, but they are *not the same*.

I wish more authors embraced this idea, because honestly, *Song of Ice and Fire* was never meant to be *a novel* (or six...seven? *whatever*). In fact, many book series (especially all those epic sci-fi/fantasy series) are just serials pretending to be "novels in a series," in my opinion.

So what *is* the difference?

Serials offer immersive, evolving narrative experiences that engage readers not just for the span of a single story arc (or season), but over months, years, or even decades. The serial fiction format employs a unique method of storytelling that capitalizes on the ongoing nature of the narrative. Instead of providing closure at the end of each book or episode, as in a traditional novel or stand-alone piece, serials thrive on continuation and evolution, which serves to keep readers (or viewers) consistently engaged. The story becomes a living, breathing entity that readers return to again and again, eager to see what new twists and turns await.

These days, a novel is considered a fictional narrative over 50,000 words long, but to my mind that is a clunky way to define it. While a novel's form is intimately related to the way the technology of books developed and therefore determined viable length (word counts, page counts, etc.), that is just one aspect of it.

As I mentioned in the Introduction, novels are a newer form of storytelling and a very codified one. That's not meant as an insult, since writing an excellent novel requires skill, talent, and experience. After all, the same is true for writing a good short story. There are breakouts (Kurt Vonnegut, I'm looking at you) but on the whole, authors are expected to work within the accepted constraints of the form.

(OFFSIDE: I know you want me to mention James Joyce's *Ulysses* here, but did you know that it is a serial? It was originally published serially from 1918 to 1920, and its structure was based on Homer's *The Odyssey* which was itself a serial, and Joyce purposefully eschewed traditional narrative structures while writing it. *So there!* Personally, I think that makes much more sense than trying to shoehorn it into a wavy-gravy "modernist novel" category. YMMV.)

The critical component of defining a novel is that it is a self-contained story with a full, complete narrative arc. A novel stands on its own as an individual work that can be read independently of any related stories. In short:

A novel is a self-contained, complete story with one single major narrative arc.

On the other hand, a serial has a *different structure* from a novel. It is *designed* to be ongoing and to take readers down alleyways and byways and come back around. A genuine *serial story* is *not* just a novel posted/published in parts, nor is it a completely unstructured chaos engine. A serial is not defined or constrained by technological limitations, since serials were originally oral forms of storytelling and are now usually digital ones. Some online serials go on for hundreds of chapters, but plenty of serials have shorter word lengths than some novels, so there is no point in claiming a story is a serial based on its word count.

At its heart, a serial owes its genesis to the ancient practice of transformative storytelling and iterative creative processes.

In short:

A serial is a generative, dynamic story.

What does that *mean?*

I know the word "generative" has taken a beating since artificial intelligence went mainstream by way of large language models (LLM), but in this case I'm not talking about A.I. at all. For something to be labeled "generative" it must have the power of creation. In this sense, a serial is a story both created (past tense) and actively being created (present tense), which determines what will be created (future tense).

That said, I have reduced usage of the word "generative" due to the confusion, and will use "dynamic" in its place from here on out.

A serial is dynamic because it is a never-ending (unstoppable!) story. It can be told in chunks, and I've already pointed out, there are many novel series that are actually serials. A couple of key components characterize a serial:

Firstly, in serial fiction, world-building is a continuous process that extends beyond a single story arc. As the story progresses, the narrative universe keeps expanding and evolving, adding new locations, societies, and cultures, or revealing previously hidden aspects of the world. This constant expansion and deepening of the narrative universe invites readers to explore and engage with the story on an ongoing basis. They don't just consume the world; they live in it, making new discoveries alongside the characters, which adds to the appeal and the sense of an "unstoppable" story.

Secondly, characters in serial fiction often have the space and time to develop and evolve in complex, realistic ways that are difficult to achieve in the novel format. Readers have the opportunity to watch characters grow, learn, and change over time, which can lead to a deeper emotional investment in their journeys. The serial format also allows for a larger ensemble cast, with multiple characters getting their own arcs and development. The continuous, unfolding nature of these character arcs helps maintain reader interest and anticipation. The desire to see what happens next to beloved characters, or how they will react to new challenges or changes, creates a narrative momentum that pulls readers from one installment to the next.

Both of those aspects lead to the one thing I warn

authors about when planning to write a serial: when you write a *true* serial, expect things to change, including your characters, the setting, the timeframe, the (for lack of a better word) *vibe*.

Great novels, of course, contain major changes to settings and timeframes, as well as feature significant character development. They *must*, in order to be great! The difference here is that a *great* **serial** has protagonists who go through *several* arcs of character (or situation) development, and often in reiterative (cyclical) ways. Diversions, prequels, sequels, and side quests are woven into the narrative in ways that give literature professors hives. This is why serials are often so very long (and why they are often accused of being too protracted, too repetitive, and too convoluted).

Take the classic portal fantasy, *The Chronicles of Narnia*. It is, in my opinion, a very good example of a serial. (I warn you now: the more you dig into this, the more it will change your perceptions about a lot of your favorite stories, both printed and visual!)

Over the course of the story, the characters change a lot. It starts as a fun romp in fantasy land in *The Lion, the Witch, and the Wardrobe*. There are hints of bigger, heavier themes to come, but not too overtly. By the time you work your way to *The Last Battle*, you are a limp rag of a human being. The children who started the story are not children anymore, and even Narnia has been revealed as a complex place laden with unhappy history. There are also books in the series that are prequels to the main storyline. There is just SO MUCH there, and it is all built out of the main story in a dynamic way that makes little sense according to traditional "novel narrative form" even if each individual story hews to classic novel structures.

You might be surprised to discover that the "books" of *Chronicles of Narnia* are, by modern standards, mostly novellas in the 40,000- word range (suitable for the young adult (YA) demographic they were written for). The whole series clocks in at a respectable 382,000 words, which is part of the reason I consider it a serial. That is too long for a traditional novel, which is usually in the 100,000- to 200,000-word range, and the story told throughout the novellas is convoluted even if each "installment" holds its own independently enough to be considered a novel. *You have to look at the whole thing.*

(I'm sure there are many ways of doing that, honestly, but the one I developed is explained at length in the Serial Beats section of this book.)

So, is the whole of "The Chronicles" a series of novels or a single serial? I vote "serial," obviously, but "series" is a tried and true and still-used model of publishing books. Some are more serial-like than others. (I think the Harry Potter series walks the line between novel series and serial, for instance.) But it boils down to distribution, in that by the mid-twentieth century, serialized storytelling had fallen out of favor and, thus, there were few ways to publish it as such. The two primary story forms were short stories and novels; most of the popular fiction magazines were only for short stories, with exceptions for the occasional serialized novella. Hence, the *Chronicles of Narnia* was published as a book series because it just made financial sense.

One way some authors (and filmmakers) have worked around the issue of lacking any distribution outlets for a serial is to do a linked trilogy (also called a connected trilogy) of a *series of trilogies* connected by characters or situation (the Mistborn series by Branden Sanderson is a good example of this; of course the most famous example is the trilogy of trilogies that make up the *Star Wars* movies).

Of course, there is a lot of wiggle room in these definitions. I'm sure someone is already pulling up their *exception to the rule* on their ereader to shake in my face, but my point here is *not* to build walls that cannot be breached. These are more like lines in the sand, etched by the ever-changing whims of the wind, the tides, and the continual shifting of the beach. A novel might turn into the starting point for a serial, and a serial can be chopped up into discrete books.

What I am sharing here is a way for authors to have more control over the long-term lifeline of their stories by deciding ahead of time if they are writing a connected series of novels or novellas or short stories, or if they are writing a genuine serial. It is even possible to change that goal midstream (not always easy, but possible!).

Tl;dr - Serials are not novels, and need to be approached differently.

That's what the rest of this book is about!

WHY SERIALS?

Why write a serial?

One may as well ask: why write a novel? Or why write a short story?

You pick the form you want to write in because something about the *form* appeals to you. Perhaps the process feels natural to you, or it may challenge you to master it (personal growth ftw!).

Sometimes, you might even make the choice *subconsciously*. A story you are already working on hits a difficult section, and you realize it would work better as a serial. The opposite case is a situation where you go through the work of setting up a serial to realize it needs to be a stand-alone novel instead.

As with other forms of storytelling, picking one form

over another is a personal choice based on a lot of factors. **There is no right or wrong way to make that choice, and to be very clear: there are no hard and fast rules in play.**

You might write a novel, decide to write a sequel that turns into an ongoing serial. You can easily pluck out parts of a serial and publish them as novellas.

While serials are an old form of storytelling, they are just now becoming popular again, thanks to the digital world where people can read stories on their mobile devices anywhere, at anytime. It is why ebooks and serial-dominant sites like Wattpad and AO3 have become so popular so quickly. People love having a story in their pocket, so to speak. Which is to say, the advantages of writing and publishing a story as a serial are still being rediscovered by writers, and the opportunities to build our own fandoms through serials will be increasing for the next few years.

If you are genuinely thinking about writing a serial, here are some solid reasons why it will benefit your career as an author:

- **Engagement (fans!):** This is honestly my favorite aspect! Serial stories are released in installments, and so can generate a lot of anticipation and excitement among readers. They eagerly await the next installment, make guesses about what is going to happen, and build a community with other readers who are invested in the story. This type of regular engagement builds a dedicated base of superfans.
- **Feedback and Adaptation:** You can gather feedback from readers between installments

and potentially adjust future segments in response to reader reactions. This could range from subtle tweaks to significant plot changes, or even just making a poll to let readers name a future secondary character. Not all authors of serials like hearing reader feedback of this sort, but if you are still new to the process, hearing what readers think about each chapter as it goes up can teach you a lot!

- **Manageable Workloads:** Writing a serialized story can feel less daunting than writing a full-length novel because the project is broken down into smaller, more manageable parts. This allows for a steady, consistent writing process rather than the intensive effort that a full-length novel might require, something akin to the difference between a cross-country hike and a 50-meter dash. This is obviously not true for all authors, but it is true for me personally, and is something I really love about serials.

- **Monetization and Publication Opportunities:** Serial stories offer unique opportunities for monetization and publication, especially as subscriptions. By attracting readers to a platform that allows them to purchase paid subscriptions, such as Ream, Substack, or Patreon, you can make a comfortable living doing what you love without the worry of trying to beat algorithms or best-seller lists. If the series is popular, you could also publish collections of the installments as full-length books, either through a traditional publisher or directly as a self-published author (more on that in the Serials in Practice section).

- **Creative Experimentation:** A lesser-known benefit of writing serials is that the format allows you to experiment with narrative forms, character arcs, and plot structures. For example, you might try out different narrative voices in each installment or use the episodic structure to explore various subplots or themes. If they are not popular or you do not enjoy writing them, you just steer back to what you and your readers like.
- **Now for the best reason to write a serial, imho:** It's fun!

It is common for authors used to writing novels to be wary of the serial format. Often, they start with serializing their novels, or stringing together some short stories, but then as they become more acclimated to the pace and get reader feedback on the episodes they've published, they start drifting toward writing longer story arcs with more interwoven elements, such as a larger ensemble cast or extended time spans.

For me, acknowledging that I was really trying to write serials all along was a tremendous step up for me as a professional author. The fact that I stumbled over this insight at a time when the technology is mature enough to allow me to have it is coincidence, or perhaps more along the lines of synchronicity. Deciding to stop trying to squish my stories down into pre-determined novel formats and to accept serials as my primary writing style has revitalized my career.

If you've thought about trying your hand at writing a serial story, now is the time!

TYPES OF SERIALS

When you are in the ideation/planning stages of your serial, it will help you plan your beats structure if you first decide on the type of serial you want to write.

I have identified three primary types of serials, and while this breakdown is not "academically rigorous," they cover the majority of serial stories out there. Consider them *very large buckets* with a lot of variety! The purpose of deciding which type of serial you will write is to give you direction for which beat structure(s) to choose.

Here are the three primary types of serials:

- **Heroic serials:** the main protagonist is central throughout story arcs.
- **Episodic serials:** the protagonist changes for each season or story arc.
- **Ensemble serials:** multiple protagonists but setting/theme is consistent.

These are not meant to be used to draw strict lines around your serial story, however. Each style can contain elements of another, such as when an episodic serial has a character who serves as an anchor for introducing each season's main protagonist but who is not the one experiencing the story arc. In the Episodic Serials section, I provide Jan Karon's beloved Mitford series as a good example of this technique. Most ensemble serials use the tack of focusing on a specific character for chapters/episodes, even if they are not true episodic serials.

Any of these three serial types can also feature complex character arcs *or* flat character arcs (to be explained later!) and can be used in every fiction genre. It is also theoretically possible to start your serial as one type but morph into another as you go along (I say "theoretically" because I personally don't know of any, but if you do, please email me and tell me about it!).

Heroic Serials

The main protagonist is central throughout story arcs, whether as a loner or in the midst of a large ensemble cast; usually from their singular POV (1st or 3rd person) but not always.

Examples: *Great Expectations, Grandmaster of Demonic Cultivation*, most LitRPG, a lot of manga, *Lord of the Rings*

Heroic serials are probably what comes to most people's minds when they think of saga-length epics. You have the hero who you stick with through thick and thin. Not that such stories are always from the hero's point of view, or that the hero must be in *every* scene. Secondary characters can abound, and you can even shift into their points of view as you go along. The examples given above provide lots of instances of this.

But whatever else may happen, the *core* of the story is the hero's story. They are always the main protagonist.

The allure of this kind of story is not the hero, per se, but the hero's journey (heheheh, see what I did there!) through the story. However, writing a heroic serial means committing to the change that will result from everything the hero goes through, good and bad. While the heroic serial often leads the main character on a journey of self-discovery, where they end up wiser, more mature, and finding peace or satisfaction in life, that is not always necessary nor required.

The epic, long running manga *Berserk* (begun 1989 and

still ongoing) features a protagonist, Guts, who starts off as a tough but idealistic young warrior, but after enduring numerous tragedies, hardships, and betrayals, becomes a much more cynical character. As the series progresses, Guts develops an intense bitterness and anger, but also a sense of determination and resilience. However, the journey Guts goes through is not a straightforward transition from idealism to cynicism. His character development is complex and multifaceted, shaped by a myriad of experiences and relationships.

Likewise, Frodo's journey in LotR has an undercurrent of tragedy, and by the end of the story, he is a much different person than how he started as a sweet young hobbit who craved adventure.

Claire in *Outlander* (the book series, which is arguably a serial in my opinion) experiences many profound and often traumatic events which help her build personal strength and resilience. The story is ongoing, but at the time of this writing, Claire is shown as someone who has found a place and time where she feels at home and has established a loving and supportive family. The story has several very strong characters, but it always orbits Claire's journey.

A heroic serial *can* have a flat character arc, but that requires putting a different kind of story scaffolding around the protagonist. I discuss options for how to do this in the Long Arcs section.

Episodic Serials

Focus on an ensemble group, a location, or a theme, but the *primary* protagonist changes for each season or story arc.

Examples: Romance book series based on families or

a town; YA book series based on a school or club; *Bridgerton* drama; anthology television shows (e.g., *American Horror Story*, *Black Mirror*); composite novels (short stocyclescle).

The most common form of episodic serials these days is the romance book series focused on a group of people, where each novel in the series focuses on the romantic journey of a different character. Examples include romance series which are about a group of brothers or sisters, or a group of patrons of a particular diner/store/club. The current *Bridgerton* television drama, where each season has a different main couple and several side pairings, is an episodic serial. Many YA series (famously, *Sweet Valley High*) take this form.

Alternatively, episodic serials can take the form of anthology stories, where each chapter (or television episode) consists of an entirely unique story around a main theme. The television show *Black Mirror* is a good example of this, as is the legendary *Twilight Zone* franchise.

I would even include the beloved novel and short story series *Mitford* by Jan Karon under this category. Set in the (fictional) small Southern town of Mitford, North Carolina, the titular main character of the series is the Episcopal priest, Father Timothy, but each story focuses on different characters in his orbit. It is a great example of a serial where the main character experiences change and personal growth but does not have a dramatic, world-saving, superhero arc, and where the *protagonists* of the stories change depending on whatever small town drama Father Tim is dealing with.

Episodic serials are a great way for authors outside of strict genre boundaries to explore characters and settings while building a cohesive, expanding story-world that invites readers in to stay.

Ensemble Serials

Multiple protagonists, but setting/theme is consistent.

Examples: Television soap operas, space operas, *Friends, Game of Thrones, Chronicles of Narnia*

When writing this section, I decided pretty quickly that the best example of an ensemble serial is the TV show *Friends*. I have to be honest, though: I have never watched the show! However, I know all about it, and the characters, and the quirky naming convention of the episode titles, and the actors, and…well, you can't have been an adult in the late 1990s without the show infiltrating your consciousness.

It is mostly a flat character arc show, although as it went on through the years a few characters did get some character arcs of their own (character *growth?* Debatable! …let the firefights begin!). Yet, it is undoubtedly an *ensemble* show and is considered one of the few genuine ensemble shows on television up to that time. Previously, shows known for their ensemble casts (for example, the classic television show *M*A*S*H*) usually still had one or two characters who served as nominal leads the others orbited.

In an ensemble serial, the feature that connects the characters can be the setting (Manhattan; mobile hospital unit; starship), a family or organization (Lannisters and Starks; mafia; military unit), or a unique situation (zombie apocalypse; genetic mutation; alien invasion).

Ensemble stories are a great choice for serials because the rotating cast not only throws a wide net to grab readers' interests but the multiple, intertwined plots/sub-plots can carry the story along for many, many seasons.

The one troublesome issue about writing an ensemble serial is the long arc. In the next section, I will go into detail about how to choose long arcs, but keep in mind for now that a long arc for an ensemble serial might be better focused on a *situation arc* or a *group arc* rather than focusing on the arc(s) of only one or two characters.

TWO

Serial Beats

THE SPREADSHEET

The genesis for this book was a nondescript spreadsheet I created for myself in 2019, which I talked about in My Search for a Concept. I will reference The Spreadsheet and use screen snippets of it throughout this section of the book.

Click here to view the spreadsheet in Google Docs

You can copy it to your Google Drive to modify it for your own personal needs, and to use as a reference. **It is free to use, and you can share the link with anyone who you believe might find value in it.** If you find it helpful, consider supporting me by buying more of my books or signing up as a subscriber on my blog, the Scriptorium or my Serial Nation patreon!

In May, 2023, I posted a link to the old version in the Facebook Group Subscriptions for Authors (disclaimer: it is operated by the owners of Ream), and it became a smash hit of a post. The CEO of Ream at the time, Micheal Evans (he has since moved on), hosted a podcast with his business partner and Ream co-founder Emilia Rose. He asked if I wanted to do a pop-up event to discuss the topic and *two days later* (!!!) we held a well-attended webinar where I hashed out what it was, how to use it, and my thoughts on what makes a "serial."

The Spreadsheet is free to use and copy because I am very much of the opinion that information should be free (I'm a librarian, what do you expect?). However, the questions I got during that webinar about The Spreadsheet made me realize that a more in-depth explanation was needed, and that is when I decided to write a book to help people put the whole thing into practice. The title, *Become an Unstoppable Storyteller,* came from my friend and fellow subscription author Gina Hogan Edwards! <3

As I wrote this book to explain The Spreadsheet, I quickly discovered that it was missing a lot of information. After all, I originally created it for my own personal use, and so had no need to explain it to myself! I returned often to The Spreadsheet while writing to update and clarify terms, so the current version of it is very different from the original. Turns out once I explained one thing, a cascade of other changes resulted!

I'll use screen snippets of The Spreadsheet where applicable, but I highly recommend having it available as you read through this book. I consider it a "living document" that I will continue to refine and expand, so even after you make a copy for yourself, I invite you to revisit it regularly.

Serial Nation

Time moves on, and in 2026 I have expanded the work of this book and The Spreadsheet into a whole movement! You can find us on Substack, join my Patreon, or join one of my hands-on cohorts which I hold multiple times a year. The cohort is designed to help authors launch their serials, so if you are still waffling about it, consider signing up! Visit Serial Nation website for links and more information!

BEATS, OUTLINES, AND WRITING OFF A CLIFF

Many people think serials are the provenance of discovery writers (a.k.a. pantsers), since quite a lot of serial authors write in what I refer to as the "au courant" method of writing, which is to write and post/publish an ongoing story before it is finished.

However, the beats method explained in this book will be useful for writing serials whether you are a planner (outliner) or a pantser (discovery writer), or fall somewhere on that spectrum.

In fact, I purposely designed it that way because I believe its most valuable feature is its *flexibility*.

As a discovery writer myself, the worst writing advice I had to get over was that stories can only be written one way: *from an outline*. It doesn't matter which type of outlining method was the "one way," since they changed over the years like any trend does. This advice was repeatedly hammered home to me when I was a young writer in the 1980s and 1990s, but I was *terrible* at it. There was no surer way to kill my ability to write a story than to outline it in any detail. It was frustrating and made me feel like a failure. If that was where the buck stopped, then I was permanently stalled at "the outlining stage."

Yet, I kept writing. I always fell back on the way I knew I could do it, which was "just to sit down and do it." Getting into fanfiction in 2007 really saved my bacon, because in that supportive and (generally) forgiving environment, I managed to get over my fear of "publishing" and just let my imagination *rip*. I wrote over one million words of fanfiction within ten years, and the experience taught me a lot about myself as a writer.

More importantly, as I wrote and branched out and the years passed, I finally met authors who use lots of different methods of writing, eventually discovering what was then called pantsing, which described my own best practices. What a revelation that was!

I've heard from a lot of writers about how they, too, stumbled over different methods and approaches for their work, which made me feel better about what I had considered my heretical ways. Fortunately, as time passed (I'm old!) it became more acceptable for authors to claim different writing approaches than what was taught in one specific textbook from the 1960s (okay, old *and* bitter! I'll own that).

What that long, drawn-out lesson taught me was that there is no One Right Way to approach writing a story. You have to choose the form (novel, serial, short story, etc.) then choose a structure that fits your method as a writer, as well as the type of story you want to write, and then do your Groove Thang. For some, that's character sheets and deep outlines. For others, that's jumping in and writing without a map.

All this meant that the whole idea of *Unstoppable Story-telling* had to be flexible. As I worked on it, I realized I needed to make sure *every* kind of author, not just pantsers like me, would find it useful in creating serial stories.

But how?

First, systems like this allow authors the freedom to explore their story without getting mired in the weeds of pacing, which is why story structures such as (the many versions of) the three-act structure, the hero's journey, and

Save the Cat!™ continue to be so popular. The structures are ostensibly fixed, but in practice, they are flexible enough so that every author can adjust them in their own way to build their stories according to their preferred approach to the writing process.

Likewise, I did not want the *Unstoppable* method to be prescriptive, but rather serve as a meta-structure that can be scaffolded with a variety of story structures that authors are already comfortable using.

Secondly, by creating a method based on beats rather than a strict outline, it sits in the middle ground between pantsers and plotters and thus can be easily picked up and used by either type of writer.

That is due to the intrinsic nature of story beats and outlines, not anything I particularly created with the *Unstoppable* method.

Here is why it works: *generally speaking*, **plotters write *from* outlines, while pantsers write *toward* beats.**

Think of it this way: plotters (outliners) build a story up from the beats, usually creating outlines and other supporting material such as character profiles as they go. Some create detailed outlines that are not too different from rough drafts, while others stick to the basic who/where/what as they put all the pieces together. Plotters like seeing the big picture in all its detailed glory. Some just want *more* details than others! The important thing that defines them is that they *start* with an outline, usually based on the beats/structure they prefer, and write out from there, building up the words to create the story around the framework of the outline and supporting materials.

Pantsers come in many flavors, but I've noticed that the most successful ones are those who tend to write *toward the beats* of a story structure, or as I describe it in my book *By the Seat of Your Pants: Secrets of Discovery*

Writing, they *write from their curiosity*. They don't know what is going to happen, necessarily, only that the next thing that *needs* to happen is "Bad Guys Close In" (Save the Cat!, beat 10). They do not want to write a story based on details pulled from an outline; they need to put in the specifics of the story first and weave their words towards a final design based on where they are going. Most pantsers will tell you that they have a general idea of how they want a story to go, or what the ending will be, they just don't know how it will get there!

I know a lot of authors, and the pantsers who claim they don't use *any* kind of structure usually write stories that, when you break them down, nonetheless follow a known story structure. They are highly intuitive writers and don't even need a beat sheet to know what is supposed to happen next! But they *do know*, even if they are not consciously aware of it.

Stories need structure (James Joyce used the Odyssey, and to each their own!), but authors need freedom to exercise their creativity within that structure. I hope my serial story beats method gives you both the versatility and the firm foundation to write *unstoppable stories*!

OVERVIEW OF UNSTOPPABLE STORYTELLING BEATS

Time for the juicy stuff!

This section will break down what I have determined are the **three most important elements** for a successful serial, based on a fair amount of research and deconstructing serials (and not-serials). Keep in mind that you don't *have* to use the *Unstoppable* beats structure for a serial. If you can drag out a long arc for 200+ chapters without any need to chunk it into more discrete parts, then blessings be upon you! (Can't be me!)

But the reason I developed this for myself originally was that I wanted beats to write toward that would be easy to keep track of and would work at a structural level to drive the story for as long as I wanted it to go.

In the following chapters, I go over each step of the system in detail, but if you want the secret sauce and no run-around, here it is, **from the top down**:

Decide on a serial type with a big plot that you know will take your character(s) a long time to work through, and map that to a story beats structure that fits the genre/story (The Long Game). Break it into seasons using acts, making sure that each season as a whole overlaps with the long arc's acts (Reasons for the Seasons). Decide on sub-plots to act as bridges (Beware the ShArcs!) between seasons by having them start after the mid-point of a season and then wrap up after the first or second chapter of the following season. Once your initial long arc is nearing completion, decide on another big plot to serve as long arc two, and start the process over again.

Ta da! You now have a serial!

I want to point out here that while I will explain this in the following sections from the top down, that is, starting with the big picture (the long arc) and drilling down into the parts that make up the whole, there are many ways to approach building a serial with beats. If you find starting with the long arc too overwhelming, work in reverse by starting with a lowly scene and building up from there to a single season's arc, then use that to discover what the long arc is (this process should be familiar if you have ever used Randy Ingermanson's Snowflake Method of story design). It really doesn't matter which order you go in, and I am only starting with an analysis of long arcs because that's how it developed when I was writing this book.

Whichever direction you come at it, if you prefer outlining your stories in detail, you can use this structure to actually outline everything you want to have happen. If you are a pantser, I have advice on how to set up a long arc that you can write to in the section about long arcs, but once you have decided on your beats, you can still *discover* away!

You can also create a serial that is about more than one protagonist, and I'll be explaining how to switch off main characters as well. This will be especially useful for romance authors using the episodic serial type who want to change the main couples after each season or long arc while keeping the serial going as a unified story.

Spoiler: A lot of the tricks you have used to create novel series based around families, communities, or locations will work here. However, there are a few small things you need to add to your plans to keep from falling into the dreaded *series void*!

Before moving on, I want to clearly identify the three most important elements of the *Unstoppable* serial beats:

- **Long arcs**, which are built around a complex story beat structure, overlap each other and run alongside both seasons and short arcs.
- **Multiple seasons**, which are built around basic or genre-specific story beat structures, comprise chapters and episodes that happen sequentially in installments.
- **Short arcs** (a.k.a. ShArcs; a type of sub-plot), which function as "bridging beats" between seasons (or other breaks in narrative), and occur

at regular intervals but do not have to overlap each other.

The two key elements here are the short arcs and long arcs because they provide two additional story structures that engage the reader outside of the regular season. Why is that important? Because **a season standing on its own with no other story structures around it is just a novel.**

One thing I want to clear up before you move on is the comparison of television seasons to serial seasons. They have a similar concept but are *not the same*.

It has become common parlance in the author community to consider a serial season as comparable to a novel's arc. Indeed, many serials get chopped up that way to be published as book series, but the structure of a whole serial season is more similar to a single television show's episode (three act structure and Save the Cat!™ being common variations). It is technically more accurate to equate a television show's season to a serial's long arc.

Likewise, what serial authors call chapters equate with chapters in novels but when compared to television show formats, equal scenes. It can get...yeah, pretty confusing.

However, if you line them up side by side, the differences are obvious:

Television	Serial	Novel
Entire Show Run	**Entire Serial Story**	
Season	Long Story Arc	
Episode	Season	**Entire Novel Story**
Scene	Chapter (Episode)	Chapter
	Scene	Scene

But at this point, the terms are settled in the general discourse and I don't want to create confusion by trying to redefine a serial season in order to appease my need for symmetry. Just be aware that when I use terms like "season" and "chapter/episode" I am referencing *the way they are used in serial stories*, not television (unless I state otherwise, of course). Likewise, I will use "chapter" predominantly as a stand-in for "season beats" unless I'm specifically talking about novels.

As mentioned earlier, in the following chapters I am going to work from the top-down, starting with long arcs since they are often the primary structure around which everything else hangs. Then we move into seasons, which explain concepts such as chapters (beats) and episodes (releases) in detail. Finally, we get to the glue that holds a bunch of parts together, the short arcs a.k.a. ShArcs (a type of sub-plot), and all the different ways you can use them to keep the story pacing snappy.

I will address the value of cliffhangers as we go along because they are important and have traditionally been the main advice for serial writers to keep readers engaged. However, the *Unstoppable Storyteller* beats system allows you a lot more flexibility. You'll still be using cliffhangers, but not exclusively, and you will be able to use a lot of different types of cliffhangers outside of immediate plot beats. I address this more comprehensively in the section Cliffhangers: Always Required, Y/N?.

Remember that the *whole point of this entire story structure* is to make your stories addictive for readers, so that they subscribe/follow/sign up for your work and help you keep writing it!

THE LONG GAME (LONG ARCS)

What is a long arc? It is probably why you want to write a serial to begin with.

You have an epic and/or sprawling tale that you *know* is going to be long, convoluted, and complex, and you are looking for ways to organize it that aren't overwhelming to you. You know that the whole story won't fit in a typical novel, and you've been considering maybe writing an old-fashioned trilogy or maybe a 3+3 series (three sets of trilogies), or simply a loosely connected "series" of novels.

Or maybe you are imagining a set of connected stories in a unique world (fantastical or historical) and want to let your readers roam through that *world of connections*, keeping them addicted for the next development, the next amazing character, without having to spend all your money on Facebook ads to lure them into buying a bunch of books.

Maybe (like me!) you've been subconsciously leaning into the serial format but have been going crazy trying to wrestle down those instincts in order to create "proper" novels.

Now you've discovered the serial form, or maybe rediscovered it, and you are ready to go!

The long arc is the skeletal structure that supports the

entire serial, so it is a good place to start planning. (Don't worry, discovery writers! You need to do very little planning, and I'll explain why in a moment). The long arc is what we refer to as the "main storyline" or the "primary plot," but it all means the same thing: **the overarching through-line of the story.**

For instance, the long arc in *The Lord of the Rings* is, obviously, Frodo's journey to destroy the ring. Yet, there is so, *so* much more driving that story along as it orbits around that primary plot.

Another example is the long arc in *The Grandmaster of Demonic Cultivation*, which is ostensibly about Wei Wuxian's sacrifice and redemption, yet that is absolutely the least of what happens in the story. It is not necessarily even *why* things happen to him, as it is a complex narrative of generational trauma, YA misadventures, war, genocide, personal tragedies, and true love. Wei Wuxian's tragic death, tragic transmigration, and eventual happy ending are the long arc around which everything else hangs.

A true long arc maps out over several seasons of a serial, at least three but up to ten or more. The long arc needs a robust beat structure, and while the classic three-act structure can work wonders, a long arc is much more compelling if you use something like the hero's journey, the virgin's promise, or ring composition/chiastic structure.

To be honest, plenty of serial long arcs don't hold to a traditional beats structure. But in the most successful ones, the ones that keep going for years and stay popular, you will likely find that the long arcs are following *some* kind of beat structure, even if you can't see it up close in individual installments of the story.

One of my favorite ongoing serials, the magnificent comic The Property of Hate (TPoH) by Sarah Jolley, has twenty-eight seasons (volumes) and is over 600 pages long, filled with a complex narrative and staggeringly brilliant art. It updates nearly every week and has been running since 2012. After all that time, though, the long arc of Hero's journey (that is actually the name of the little girl at the center of the story) is possibly at the two-thirds mark. The long arc is fairly obvious (Hero saves the world...? Somehow? Maybe? And will she ever be able to go home????), but there are a lot of twists and turns and side characters and short arcs that keep readers addicted to the story (including me). Particularly, Hero's guide/caretaker (RGB) has a slowly revealed backstory (including the mystery of whether or not he might be the *actual* protagonist of the story!) which is ongoing, and rises and falls in between major plot reveals.

It is easy to read TPoH and get involved in the current season's arc, but at the same time, you never *ever* lose sight of the story's primary objective.

You find the same thing in long-running manga like *ONE PIECE*, where "tidier" seasonal arcs are straightforward and usually kick off when the Straw Hat Pirates arrive at a new location and get into a fight. Despite all the battles, you know the goal is for the protagonist, Monkey D. Luffy, to find the magical treasure, the eponymous "one piece" of the title (more on Monkey and his crew in the next section).

The same can be said of Frodo's quest, which is always to destroy the One Ring no matter what wars happen around him. Even with Wei Wuxian, readers know that the endgame is somehow, *someway*, WangXian (iykyk).

Frodo is usually mapped to the hero's journey, and while I think it's *possible* to retroactively map Wei Wuxian roughly to that as well, *Grandmaster of Demonic Cultivation* is culturally rooted in the Chinese saga tradition (in the footsteps of the ancient *Journey to the West* or the modern wuxia works of Jin Yong). Point being, if you know what to look for, you will see *how* the long arcs wax and wane as they are woven through shorter seasons.

Because the long arc beats are so critical to the overall serial's structure, you really need to decide on them early, whether you start there or with just a single scene.

If your goal is to write a serial, then it is a bad idea to think of a plot idea and quickly jump into telling that story, because you run the risk of telling it too quickly and congratulations, you have a novel on your hands! Which you can use as a season of your serial, but then you are scrambling to find a bigger long arc to hold it together.

Don't think big, think *bigger*. Even if your plot idea is "Hannah Hero drives a car across the zombie wastelands," think of it in *enormous* terms. This might be hard if you are used to the paring knife needed to construct genre-conforming novels, and you are constantly looking for ways to eliminate settings, arcs, sub-plots, and secondary charac-ters for the sake of "tight pacing."

Instead of making it a quick trip with a few road bumps (zombies), put Hannah Hero on one side of the continent and make it necessary for her to get all the way to the other side, with every obstacle possible in between. You are not Cormac McCarthy writing *The Road*; you are Stephen King writing *The Stand*. Put everything in there, including the kitchen sink!

I know you plotters/planners are champing at the bit, excited for all the many complicated outlines you are going to create, and good for you! Can't be me, and I understand why it can't be a lot of other discovery/pantser authors.

But that's fine, because serials, like novels, don't *require* an outline if that is not how your brain works. If you are not a plotter and you don't want to be beholden to a vast, complicated outline, then simply start with Hannah Hero on one side of the continent, and begin the story there, knowing that somehow, for some reason unknown to you, *mere discovery writer*, she needs to get all the way to the other side of the continent. Then maybe also across the ocean! How far can Hannah go? Time to find out!

My silly action hero example aside, the point is that it is actually **easier to plan a long arc the more epic you make it.** Can you create a long arc based on a simple three-act structure that is focused on your protagonist trying to grow tomatoes in Florida? (Non-random example, do not judge.) Yes, you can, but the more constrained your main plot, the harder it will be to make the long arc interesting enough for readers to follow through (aside from master gardeners who really love tomatoes, perhaps).

Unlike every "how to write a novel" course ever, I am not telling you to tighten up your plot and cut out filler and delete one-third of your first draft. Quite the opposite. Please enjoy this advice for what it is, as rare as it is: GO HAM, AUTHOR!!!!

If you are thinking about a coming-of-age fantasy story, the genre convention is usually a trilogy of short novels which follow the character from about ages thirteen to their early twenties (e.g. *The Hunger Games*). You can follow the same character arc, but instead of three epic acts, one per novel, to get through their hero's journey, consider that every year in that decade of time is its own seasonal arc, within the hero's journey long arc. That means eight to ten seasons of the story!

Cozy mysteries are usually episodic in nature, in that each novel is "case opened-investigated-case shut" by the end. However, if you look at successful long-running mystery series, a longer story arc is often going on in the background, such as a romance, or family reconciliation, or the main character going through a major life change. Take a look at your protagonist and imagine her ten years down the road: what kind of changes do you want to see? Does she have a kid? Does she start a new business? Get a divorce? Go no-contact with her abusive parent? Don't wrap up any of those threads too early; instead mold them into a long story arc that can be woven through the episodic murder mysteries.

If you are more interested in writing literary fiction, or women's fiction, or other genres that are not traditionally considered as comprising "epic" material, preferring the more intricate personal stories of characters in more mundane settings, your long arc might be tied to the changing generations of a family. Colleen McCullough would approve!

I would even argue that serials are a much underutilized form for telling intimate stories about humanity and change. Not everything needs cliffhangers and dragons. Charles Dickens did pretty okay, after all.

There are literally endless stories to tell, and I can't help you decide on the ones that are important to you, but no matter what your preference, if you can find a long arc to hang it on, you can write a serial!

Non-Character Driven Long Arcs

There might be times you want to build a long arc (or two) that does not focus on a specific character. If you are planning a serial featuring a flat character arc or you plan on writing an ensemble serial, those are situations where your long arc should not be a *person*. If you are writing literary fiction (or related, like historical fiction or even memoir) then you might create a long arc based on a theme or the changes that happen in a family over several generations.

Craft a long arc showing how they went from being poor immigrants to established community members over three or four generations. You can even craft it around a theme such as the ongoing costs of generational abuse in families, or the "life" of the house they all live in. It's arguable, I think, that the Yellowstone TV show franchise (*1883*, *1923*, and *Yellowstone*, to date) fits neatly into this category, with the Dutton ranchland being the primary "protagonist" of the series.

This is definitely "hard mode" for long arc development, but not impossible! Here are two examples of how to build non-character driven long arcs: **situation arcs** and **group arcs**.

Situation Arc

Let's say you are creating a heroic serial, but the protagonist has a flat character arc. Since your main character is not experiencing their own hero's journey or similar, you need to create a situation *around* them that *is* experiencing a major change, much as in a role-playing game (RPG).

A good example of this is the classic zombie apocalypse story. Remember Hannah Hero, mentioned above? She's a classic action-adventure hero with all the skills needed to survive and is a charismatic leader out to save as many people as possible on her cross-country road trip, Furiosa-style. She's incredible, as-is, so you don't really want to write a major *character arc* around her. Instead, you can put her into a slowly unfolding zombie apocalypse, where the *situation arc* changes from various stages of mildly alarming to incredibly dangerous to (eventually) peacetime in a safe haven. The surrounding characters, some of whom she saves, some she can't, have their own dramatic arcs that give the story intensity and texture to grab readers and keep them hooked. You can even include minor character development in the season arc. The key here is to make sure the beats of the situation arc, in this case a zombie apocalypse, change regularly.

One reason LitRPG is so popular as a genre is that it commonly uses this formula and, as in popular video game franchises, can keep going for years. If you examine some of the longer running video games that are not about any kind of main character arc, what you'll usually find is a *situation arc* (which, if you *are* a gamer, is something you can also think of as *levels).*

Situation arcs are also great for ensemble serials. In the zombie apocalypse scenario, you might have several protagonists working together to travel across a zombified wasteland.

And yes, you can actually map story beats to a situation arc, although it might be easiest to keep to simple ones like a classic three-act story structure. In any case, **the situation arc is the long arc**, so you will have to consider how you are going to break it up into seasons.

In our zombie apocalypse example, each season might be a region Hannah Hero has to travel through, or you can create different antagonists for each season. There are a lot of examples of long-running stories, both novel series and television shows, that switch up antagonists as the story goes on while the long arc continues and the characters remain relatively unchanged. The advantage of changing up an antagonist is that you can use something like Save the Cat!™ for the underlying structure of the season (although that is just one of many options).

I'd argue that the *best* long-running serials are a combination of character and situation arcs! Which, when you think about it, is about 90% of long, serialized manga. ¯_(ツ)_/¯

If you are having trouble thinking of a situation as something you can map to the beats of a story structure, a good trick is to simply anthropomorphize the concept of it *as the protagonist,* as I mentioned earlier with the Dutton ranch. For instance, "if the zombie apocalypse were the lead character, what would they do next?" Well, if the next beat is "Turning Point 3: Point of No Return" (beat six in Michael Hauge's Six Stage Plot Structure), then this is where the zombie virus has reached critical mass and is spilling out into the whole human population. The next beat, which is about complications and raising the stakes, is where the military starts nuking cities to try to contain the virus, so the zombie apocalypse has to *try harder* to win. And so on!

Group Arc

A group arc treats the collective characters as an organic whole. They are all, together, traveling through the beats of the hero's journey or a ring composition/chiastic structure.

A group arc does not equal an ensemble serial, although it can, and is a particularly good choice for the type. Many examples of group arcs have an ostensible main protagonist, though.

Song of Ice and Fire (the book series) is a good example of a bunch of characters who are all on a long group arc that might be called "winter is coming." The white walkers are the true danger and quite possibly the cause of an imminent apocalypse (when is the next book coming out, again?), so all the brouhaha about the Iron Throne is very dramatic set dressing as the long arc continues apace around everyone in the story.

A lot of ensemble manga feature a group arc as the

long arc, especially ones that focus on high school and college groups on quests. One example already mentioned is *ONE PIECE* by Eiichiro Oda, which has a lead protagonist (Monkey D. Luffy) but is generally considered an ensemble story. This incredibly long-running serial launched in 1997 and is ongoing, with the long arc being the group's search for a mythic treasure ("one piece"), which, when found, will make their leader King of the Pirates. All the characters have their own arcs as the story progresses (disclaimer: I have not read the whole series), but it is the journey of the group all together that carries the serial on episode after episode. Another good example of this kind of long group arc is *My Hero Academia* by Kōhei Horikoshi.

Generational storylines fall under "group arcs," as the family's fate is shared collectively (even if, in some cases, posthumously). Plenty of successful novels are based on this set up. *One Hundred Years of Solitude* by Gabriel García Márquez is, in my opinion, definitely a novel and *not* a serial, but if you consider the themes of the story (namely, the cyclic repetition of tragedy as shown through seven generations of a single family), it is easy to see how they serve as the long arc for the story.

Beat Structures for Long Arcs

You can use any beat structure for long arcs, but the more complex they are, the better. The following is a selection of story/beat structures that lend themselves well to long arcs:

- **Hero's Journey:** Popularized by Joseph Campbell's work, the Hero's Journey comprises stages like the call to adventure, refusal of the call, crossing the threshold, trials, the ordeal, the reward, the return, and the transformation.

- **Heroine's Journey:** Based on Maureen Murdock's work, it's a female-centric version of the Hero's Journey, focusing on personal growth and relationships.

- **Ring Composition/Chiastic Structure:** a narrative technique that involves a story being told in a circular structure, where the ending mirrors the beginning, and key points along the way reflect each other. The basic beats are represented as A-B-C-B-A.

- **Romancing the Beat:** A genre-specific story structure for romance novels by Gwen Hayes with four acts and 20 beats.

- **Six Stage Plot Structure:** Michael Hauge's three-act structure that alternates beats between six stages and five turning points.

- **Story Circle:** Created by Dan Harmon, this story structure is a simplified version of the Hero's Journey, consisting of eight stages.

- **Tragedy Structure:** Popular in ancient Greek drama and later in Shakespeare's tragedies, these stories typically follow the downfall of the main character, often in a three- or five-act structure.

- **Virgin's Promise:** Created by Kim Hudson, this story structure is about a character stepping into their power and potential, often used in coming-of-age stories. It is based on the classic Hero's Journey and contains three acts with thirteen beats.

REASONS FOR THE SEASONS

As explained in the Overview, the term "season" has been co-opted from television by the writing community to refer to collections of chapters in serials, which are often how they are later published as books. Essentially, a *season* is a convenient way to break up a longer story to make it more manageable.

But what is a season, and why do we have them at all?

In the early days of television (and I do mean *early*, in the 1940s), the traditional "broadcast season" aligned with the school year, beginning in the fall and ending in late spring with summer being the off-season. This schedule was a holdover from radio, but it was also influenced by other industries. For example, the automotive industry introduced new car models in the fall, and they wanted to advertise those on television. Additionally, families watched less television over the summer as it was a popular time for vacation travel, so networks would wait until the fall to debut their most promising new shows.

In the era of streaming and digital media, the concept of "a season" has shifted, with some series dropping all episodes of a season at once, and others running new seasons year round without summer breaks. The length of a season varies as well, with some streaming shows only having six to ten episodes per season, while traditional network shows may have 20 or more. When I started watching Chinese dramas, I had a bit of dissonance since the particular dramas I was watching were often very long (50+ episodes) and were not broken up into discrete seasons like I was used to. (To be sure, a lot of Asian dramas, especially Korean and Japanese dramas, are shorter overall. One of my favorite sweet danmei/boy love shows, the South Korean drama *Semantic Error,* is only eight episodes long.)

So that's where the concept of a season comes from, but how is it useful for serials?

The power of building your basic layer of storytelling around a season is that you can use a beat structure that will keep readers engaged from chapter to chapter while the long story arc is strung out across multiple seasons.

Whether you are using the Save the Cat!™ or Romancing the Beat, tying a chapter to a beat gives your readers a narrative arc to follow. Think of serial beats the same you do novel chapters: both as structural tools for storytelling and lures to keep readers hooked.

If you want your seasons to be published as a book series down the road, and you are using a short beat structure, then you might realize quickly that keeping chapters at 2,000 words or so in order to post them as episodes to your readers will end up with a very short book, or long novella. If that is not what you want, you either have to write longer chapters or you need to break them apart into scenes and post the scenes as episodes.

It seems super basic to explain what scenes are to a bunch of writers, but just so we are all on the same page: a scene is merely a discrete part of a chapter, often used to mark the passage of time, location, or a change of POV (or all three). A whole chapter can be one scene, or a chapter can be made up of multiple scenes.

What confuses people is that most serialization sites (RoyalRoad, Wattpad, Ream, to name but a few) refer to each episode as a chapter because they have flattened the whole internal structure of stories. When you are trying to plan your story and you are going back and forth between the layered novel structure of "Manuscript > Parts > Chapters > Scenes" versus the flat serial structure these sites use of "Story > Chapters" where "chapters" are actually "installments," it can be utterly bewildering.

I write in Scrivener, a great tool for writers that is so much more than a mere word processing app. It allows for an incredibly complex organization of stories and is designed with the traditional "layered" format of novels in mind. Here is a comparison of how the same story, my novel *The Queen's Aerie,* looks in Scrivener, on the left, and in Ream, on the right. In Scrivener, there is a separate prologue, and the first two chapters have scenes "nested" under them and color-coded to reflect which character's POV the scene is from; while in Ream each individual scene is a separate episode (installment). There are no "chapters" in sight and scenes have been renamed to appeal to readers:

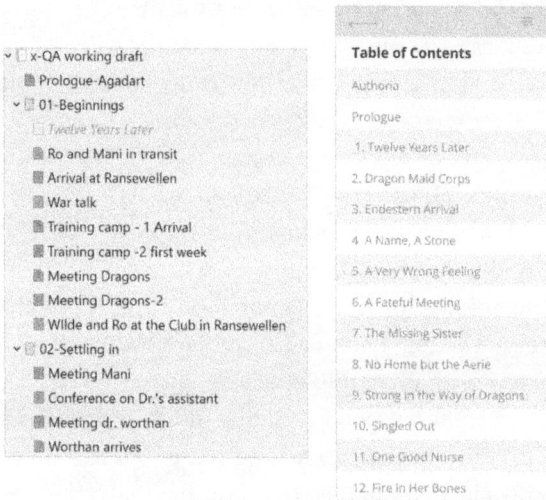

x-QA working draft	Table of Contents
Prologue-Agadart	Authoria
01-Beginnings	Prologue
Twelve Years Later	1. Twelve Years Later
Ro and Mani in transit	2. Dragon Maid Corps
Arrival at Ransewellen	3. Endestern Arrival
War talk	4 A Name, A Stone
Training camp - 1 Arrival	5. A Very Wrong Feeling
Training camp -2 first week	6. A Fateful Meeting
Meeting Dragons	7. The Missing Sister
Meeting Dragons-2	8. No Home but the Aerie
Wilde and Ro at the Club in Ransewellen	9. Strong in the Way of Dragons
02-Settling in	10. Singled Out
Meeting Mani	11. One Good Nurse
Conference on Dr.'s assistant	12. Fire In Her Bones
Meeting dr. worthan	
Worthan arrives	

This will probably change in the future as serialization platforms develop and expand their features for both writers and readers, but in the meantime, it means you do not have any way of identifying separate seasons in your serial, unless you include that in each episode's title (e.g., "Arc 2, Chapter 10: Mister Ed Joins the Army").

That's a long way to say that most serial story platforms commonly use "chapter," "scene," and "episode" as interchangeable terms for the smallest individual installment of a story that gets posted sequentially.

In the case of *The Queen's Aerie*, the original novel of nine chapters comprising four to six scenes each, along with a prologue and epilogue, was restructured to be serialized in 59 installments (chapters/episodes).

For the sake of designing a story based on beats, just remember that **chapters match the season's beats while episodes are installments which get posted serially** (which means an episode might be a whole chapter, or it might be scenes from within a chapter as happened with *The Queen's Aerie*).

When I talk about chapters in regard to serials, they have nothing to do with how the story is formatted for delivery but rather are significant because they are story beats within a season. In the image below, a single season (season 1) is broken up into the primary acts, the chapters (beats), and, in this case, each chapter is an episode (installment):

Season #	Acts	Chapters (beats)	Episodes (installments)
1	Act 1: Set Up	Beginning	1
1		Inciting Incident	2
1		Set up climax	3
1	Act 2: Confrontation	Obstacle Introductin	4
1		Midpoint	5
1		Obstacle confrontation	6
1		Disaster/Crisis	7
1	Act 3: Resolution	Climax	8
1		Denouement	9
1		Ending	10

Seasons are critical for determining the ultimate length of a serial since the word count of the chapters decides the total wordcount. It is *possible* to work backward from a long arc word count goal, but in the end, you'd still have to do the math to decide how long each chapter (beat) is and collectively how long each season is. Keep in mind that if you plan to eventually publish your serial (or parts of it) as a book series, the seasons are the most convenient format to break into individual books.

If you are determined to write a long arc that is 300,000+ words long and you are using the hero's journey structure of three acts/thirteen beats for it, then each *long arc act* would come in roughly at 100,000 words and each beat would need approximately 23,000 words (I cannot believe you people are making me do *math!!!!*). Since you would space them out over several seasons, though, the *actual* determining factor on how long an *episode* (installment) is would depend on the beats structure you use for each season, which probably would *not* be the hero's journey arc (as it is one of the more complicated story beat structures out there).

If you use a basic three-act story structure for the seasons, each season would have about ten beats. If you spread the long arc's first act (100,000 words) across the ten three-act story structure of the first season (i.e., 10 beats) then the chapters would be 10,000 words long...still on the longer side, but that could work, depending on your readers and your brand. Some readers love getting long, juicy chapters, and if that is your readers, then you are done planning and ready to write!

But you also have the option of **chopping chapters (beats) into scenes and posting the scenes as installments.** This gives a bit more flexibility in episode length, as you can make them as short as 500 words or up to 5,000 words, depending on how your scenes break up the chapter. Continuing the example, with chapters of 10,000 words, you could chop them up into episodes in a lot of ways:

- Two 5,000-word scenes
- Four 2,500-word scenes
- One 3,000-word scene + two 3,500-word scenes
- Ten 1,000-word scenes
- Varying lengths, depending on pacing

If you need a visual representation of carrying beats over multiple episodes, here you go. This is **a completed first season** of a serial using a traditional three-act beats structure for both the season and the long arc:

Season	Acts	Chapters (beats)	Episodes (scenes)	Long Arc Acts	Long Arc Beats
1	Act 1 - Set Up	Beginning	1	Act 1 - Set Up	Beginning
1		Inciting Incident	2		
1			3		
1			4		
1		Set up Climax	5		
1			6		
1	Act 2 - Confrontation	Obstacle Introduction	7		Inciting Incident
1			8		
1			9		
1			10		
1			11		
1		MIDPOINT	12		
1		Obstacle Confrontation	13		
1			14		
1		Disaster/Crisis	15		
1			16		
1			17		
1		Climax	18		
1	Act 3 - Resolution	Climax continues	19		
1			20		
1			21		
1		Dénouement	22		
1		Ending	23		

This is adapted from The Spreadsheet, by the way. I simplified it a little for use here, so look at the actual spreadsheet to see how this plays out in a lot more depth. But it's probably pretty clear by now *why* I had to build a spreadsheet for this!

Take a moment to study this carefully. Here are a few points worth noticing:

- How the acts of the season and the acts of the long arc are spaced out.
- The way the start of the season's act two, "Obstacle introduction," matches up with the start of the second beat of the long arc's act one. The season's obstacle and the long arc's

inciting incident could be the same event! That's not required, as you could drop the long arc's inciting incident anywhere in the season's acts, but it is a handy way to overlap the plot points.

- How far apart the long arc beats are throughout the episodes. Readers won't even get to beat three of the long arc until season two.

- How some of the season's chapters (beats) only need one episode but others take up multiple episodes. There are no rules here, so the number of episodes is determined by the length of a particular beat.

If you're a plotter, this is an easy matter of plugging in the numbers to determine the episode lengths you need.

If you are a pantser, like me, it comes down to looking ahead to the next beat and deciding if you want to get there fast or slow, and being aware that you'll likely have shorter and longer chapters as you go along. (Personally, I find this represents a bit of freedom, as I'm not constrained to trying to make every episode the same length; however, it means I need to communicate with my readers up front that episodes will vary in length.)

While there's no requirement to plan your serial with seasons, they are *critical* for making long serials manageable for both you and your readers. Not using seasons as a framework to hold the story together over the extended journey of the long arc puts a lot more pressure on you as an author to keep each episode of the long arc engaging enough to hold readers' attention.

Beat Structures for Seasons

Let's look at a dozen or so story/beat structures that are great to use for *seasons*. You can marry one and use it over and over, or you can play around using different ones for each season. There are a lot more beat structures out in the big wide world; these are some of the most popular.

- **Dramatic Arc (Freytag's Pyramid):** Based on the analysis of Greek and Shakespearean drama, Gustav Freytag developed a five-part model: exposition, rising action, climax, falling action, and denouement.
- **Fichtean Curve:** A story structure that includes a series of crises within the narrative to keep tension high.
- **Five-Act Structure:** Seen in many of Shakespeare's plays, this structure expands the middle part of the three-act structure into three parts of its own (Rising Action, Climax, Falling Action).
- **Hollywood Formula:** A screenplay three-act structure that revolves around three main characters—the protagonist, the antagonist, and the relationship character.
- **Invisible Ink:** a very simple no-act structure consisting of seven beats developed by Brian McDonald.
- **Kishōtenketsu:** A four-act structure used widely in traditional Chinese, Korean, and Japanese narratives, focusing less on conflict and more on contrast and variation.
- **Romancing the Beat:** A genre-specific story

structure for romance novels by Gwen Hayes with four acts and 20 beats.

- **Save the Cat!:** A screenplay storytelling structure coined by Blake Snyder, with three acts and fifteen distinct plot points (beats) throughout the narrative.
- **Save the Cat! Writes a Novel:** The original Save the Cat! structure modified with permission by Jessica Brody for use with novels.
- **Save the Cat for Television Episodes:** a storytelling structure by Joel Silberman, based on Blake Snyder's classic Save the Cat with minor adjustments to fit standard 1-hour drama formats.
- **Sequential Act Structure:** Often used in episodic storytelling like TV series, where each episode has a self-contained story but contributes to the overall story arc.
- **Seven-Point Story Structure:** This structure, outlined by Dan Wells, includes seven pivotal points (beats).
- **Six Stage Plot Structure:** Michael Hauge's three-act structure that alternates beats between six stages and five turning points.
- **Snowflake Method:** Randy Ingermanson's approach to writing a novel, where the story begins with a simple premise and expands into a full plot, like a snowflake forming.
- **Story Circle:** Created by Dan Harmon, this story structure is a simplified version of the Hero's Journey, consisting of eight stages.
- **Three-Act Structure:** This is one of the simplest and most common story structures. It consists of Setup (Act I), Confrontation (Act II),

and Resolution (Act III). There are numerous versions of this structure with various numbers of beats to them.

BEWARE THE SHARCS!

Why "**ShArcs**"?

As I mentioned in the The Spreadsheet, this whole book started as a pop-up webinar I did with (then) Ream co-founder Michael Evans. I kept stumbling over saying "short arcs" and made a joke about calling them "ShArcs" and it stuck! My best friend has even suggested creating a shark mascot, which I haven't…YET!

The concept of ShArcs might seem odd at first, but they are very simple plot devices: **they are there to bridge the beats between the end of one season and the start of another.**

The assumption is usually that the long arc will serve as the overarching bridge to carry readers along in the serial even when an individual season reaches its conclusion. While that can be true, it also puts a lot of pressure on you as the writer to always make sure the long arc is front and center, even when sometimes it shouldn't (or can't) be. Long arcs have their own pacing and beats, and since that pacing is being drawn out over multiple seasons, there will be natural lags where it is simply simmering in the background. The longer the long arc, the harder you have to work to make sure everything is always dialed up to eleven.

A ShArc keeps readers invested in the story no matter where the season wraps up within the extended beats of the long arc.

So what *is* a ShArc, then? Simple: it is a *type* of subplot. What you need to keep in mind is that **every short**

arc is a subplot, but not every subplot is a short arc.

You can use secondary characters, side quests, side locations, and side situations for your short arcs, because anything that works as a subplot can be put into service as a short arc.

For example, let's say your hero has a psychic alien cat she's bonded with (you military sf fans will know who I mean!) and right before the climax of a season, the cat is kidnapped. The hero can't just break off from the primary plot at such a critical point to go search for her cat, but it is a big emotional arc throughout the end of the season: she doesn't have her psychic companion, and it makes her worried, especially since maybe she can "sense" that it is in danger, or scared, or lost. This is going on while the big space battle is raging, so readers are going to be *invested* in what is happening to the alien cat. Then the season ends with the hero flying away in triumph from the detritus of the space battle to *go! Find! Her! CAT!*

(If you do this, I guarantee your fans will be howling at you for the next season NOW, and that is honestly the *best feeling in the world!* Because we are authors and we love our cliffhangers, bwahahahahah!)

Season two starts with her embroiled in rescuing her cat, which can be part of the inciting incident that kicks off season two by introducing a new villain. And away you go!

That is a very simple example of how a short arc can carry readers into the next season, whether the long arc is able to do so or not.

The value of ShArcs is that they allow the emotional payoff of the season to wrap up in full while still dragging the reader into the next season and further along the long arc's progress. The danger of ending a season with a cliffhanger tied to the season's beats is that readers can become frustrated with the lack of closure. Instead, you are putting a lower-stake cliffhanger on offer that is important to the plot, or to the characters, but won't leave the reader feeling like they've been bamboozled.

A great example of this is provided by John Gaspard, who wrote The Popcorn Principles: A Novelist's Guide to Learning from the Movies. He talks about the *Back to the Future* series, and while this is not an example of a short arc in action, it does show the importance of wrapping up a season's complete story arc (in this case, read "season" for "movie").

The first movie ends on the high note of Marty McFly dropping back into the future (back where he started) to find everything changed for the better. All the loose ends and character arcs have been neatly wrapped up in a bow. If the movie had ended at that point, no one would complain. However, it doesn't; Doc Brown shows up and explains to Marty that his future kids are in trouble and need their help. They jump into the DeLorean and drive off into the sequel!

The sequel, however, ends on a wisp of a promise. If you don't remember, Marty manages to undermine Biff (his nemesis) so that the terrible future of 2015 (I feel *really old* right now) never happens, but it is incredibly unfulfilling because nothing was actually resolved on screen. Marty did stop the future from happening, but in the meantime, Doc Brown has disappeared, which is the cliffhanger. Gaspard explains that this is a true cliffhanger that leaves viewers dissatisfied with the movie, because the emotional arc of the story is erased with the future reset to where it started in 1985 (oh, these timey-wimey stories!), with Doc Brown in some kind of unknown state and possibly in danger.

Point being, if you, like me, were sitting in the theater in November 1989, and the final installment of the series was not coming out until May 1990, you were pretty freakin' annoyed. It was completely the opposite reaction I had to the end of the first movie. Did I go see the third movie six months later? Of course I did (*everyone* did), but I felt pretty salty about it. No shade meant to those who love the second movie, but for me, it had simply failed on the last lap. (Not really sure how they could have done it differently, since the *whole point* was for Marty to change/erase the terrible future, but still, it was very unfulfilling.)

ShArcs help you avoid that kind of situation. If you can't have Doc Brown busting into the very last scene of your story to drag people into the next season (and who can?), then a ShArc is a good stand-in.

I am often asked, though: **are all ShArcs short?**

No, they do not have to be short, but the point of a ShArc is that it is a tight enough narrative that it does not need to be broken out into beats to stay coherent for the reader (and the writer, to be honest).

For instance, in the psychic pet cat example I used above, the sub-plot is based on a complex relationship that spans most if not all of the story (the military officer being the story's protagonist, after all, and she loves her psychic cat companion), but it is a very simple setup in and of itself: the cat mysteriously disappears, the military officer is worried about it throughout a bunch of climatic battles, then heads off to parts unknown to find her cat once the season is wrapped up.

You may have a subplot(s) that weave(s) through many seasons of a long arc; one may have its own beats that you could repurpose to use as a short arc.

A good example of this is the classic mentor arc, which is common in fantasy and LitRPG stories. The hero finds their mentor in the first act, usually goes through their training montage somewhere in the second act, and then, of course, the mentor dies heroically while protecting or defending the hero in the third act. The mentor's story is a subplot, and you can mine it in multiple ways to explain the backstory (Obi-Wan Kenobi) or to develop world-building that the hero might not see or understand (Gandalf).

The ShArc might be the launch of the subplot itself, where the hero meets their mentor via some kind of side quest. If you state the need for the side quest right before the final climactic chapter of the season, then end the season with an episode in which the hero is on the side quest and, OH NO, FALLS INTO A TRAP! WHO IS THE DASTARDLY PERSON WHO BUILT THE TRAP? End the scene with a menacing character standing over our hero, who is then revealed in the next season's first installment as the mentor who is testing the hero's skills. Reuse and repurpose the mentor arc as needed as you go along!

While I've read a lot of serial stories in my life, I did not solidify my ideas around ShArcs until I was watching the greatest television show ever made, the Chinese drama *Nirvana in Fire* (2015). The episodes did not hold together the way I was used to with "(Western) TV show episode" beats, often ending abruptly in the middle of a quiet scene such as a couple of characters drinking tea. Yet, I could not hit "play" fast enough to get to the next episode!

I realized quickly what the director was doing: he started and ended dramatic story arcs *in the middle of the episode*. It is something I subsequently noticed a lot of longer Chinese dramas do, although I am not educated enough on the topic of Chinese narrative beats to know if this is a carryover from classic literary forms. (If anyone reading this knows something about that, please let me know!)

While those were not short arcs, technically speaking, it sparked the idea of starting an arc in the middle of a bigger arc in order to grab readers and pull them along to the next season of the serial.

In the case of *Nirvana in Fire*, the long arc is compelling, since it is about secret identities and betrayal and revenge, and *so, so much trauma*. Yet, as keen as I was to see how the main character succeeded in his plans, there were so many subplots going on that it would have been easy to just get bored and fall out of the story completely once a subplot was wrapped up. Yet you can't, because the subplots never end when an episode ends. To get to the end of a subplot, you *must* keep watching, no matter how quietly the episodes end and start, and no matter at what point in the long arc of Mei Changsu's revenge that the episode sits.

One thing I want to stress here is that short arcs are *not required* for every season, and ShArcs should be short but can vary in length. **Their whole, entire purpose is to serve as a bridge to carry readers from one season (or long arc) to another, so there is no One Right Way to Do It.**

Sidenote: A longer subplot is also really useful for creating extra bonus scenes for your followers, or even launching off into a completely new but connected story (such as prequels, or giving a secondary character their own turn as a protagonist).

Cliffhangers: Always Required, Y/N?

I want to address one of the most common pieces of advice given to authors who are looking to write serials, which is to use cliffhangers at the end of every chapter. There is a lot of history behind the advice, since having a cliffhanger is a tried-and-true method of luring readers into buying the next episode of the story. Pulp fiction authors would approve!

However, cliffhangers are not *imperative* in ongoing serials, in general. What determines whether you need to use cliffhangers at the end of every episode boils down to how your author business is structured, and more importantly, which platforms you are posting your serials on. Furthermore, a cliffhanger can be an emotional/psychological moment of suspense; they do not always need to about physical danger.

Putting on my "history of text technology" cap again, I want to point out the phrase I used in the first paragraph: *luring readers into buying the next episode*. The whole point of the advice given to authors about cliffhangers is to encourage readers to spend money to get the next section of the story. There is a historical reason for that.

In the past, stories were published in magazines that needed to be *purchased* with each new issue in order to keep up with the story and to find out what happens next. The publisher (who was paying the author) relied on that to make money.

The anticipation was often extreme, so much so that in 1841, readers of Charles Dickens' serial *The Old Curiosity Shop* stormed the wharf where the ship transporting it was docked in order to get at the final installment. That image has always stuck with me, because it reminds me of the lines I stood in as a child outside the movie theater waiting to see every new Star Wars movie (in my case, the original trilogy, because I'm *old*!).

The reason the advice "end each chapter/episode/scene with a cliffhanger!!!!" has been ubiquitous for serial fiction authors is that during the past 200+ years, readers were required to fork out money to get a story's next installment, whether that was an issue of a magazine or the next book in a series. This scarcity model worked very well for publishers, and less well for authors.

This is the historical model of traditional publishing in a nutshell: publishers take a gamble on a story, invest money in producing it for readers to buy, and authors get paid a fraction of the profit that the publisher eventually pulls in, *and* get paid last (advances notwithstanding, as they are deducted from future revenue). When publishing houses' profit drops, the reverse is true: the first one to *not* get paid is the author.

Subscription platforms like Kindle Unlimited, Webnovel, and online comics sites such as Webtoons continue this tradition because they pay authors based on the number of reads their story gets, which sounds fair on the surface. However, it doesn't matter to the publisher *which* story the readers spend time on, because they have already paid the publisher via their *subscription to the platform*. This strongly motivates authors to make sure readers stay with *their* story through thick and thin in order to get even a tiny piece of the pie...or more accurately, the crumbs of the pie.

Because these sites act as intermediaries between the readers and the authors, they can dictate what gets read (via algorithms sorting stories by popularity and profit) and the payouts that authors get (exactly how this is done varies from platform to platform, but in general, the platforms are paid by the reader directly, which then portions out payments to authors depending on a variety of variables that are never based on "is this fair to the author?"). The motivation for authors to put extreme cliffhangers at the end of *every* episode is directly tied to how much money they might be granted by the owners of the platforms. It becomes a matter of "thrive or starve" for the authors, and cliffhangers become mandatory.

But serials don't *need* to work that way, these days.

The difference is that the technology exists now for readers to *directly* support an author with an ongoing subscription. It remains true that if you are trying to lure new readers in hopes that they become paid subscribers, you need to use a dramatic cliffhanger to get their attention and eventually their subscription. You also need to be mindful of keeping subscribers engaged with your work long term, but with a subscription business model, the need to constantly lure readers into paying to read the next installment is less of a pressure.

That is how it works for authors using subscription platforms like Ream, Substack, and Patreon. There is always a valid incentive to do everything possible to keep readers addicted to the story, but on the other hand it is not absolutely necessary. These platforms encourage a 1:1 relationship between the reader and the author, where the reader becomes a direct supporter of the author. These platforms have reversed the model: they get a payout that is a percentage of the money people are paying for subscriptions to specific writers.

In other words, readers are *already* invested in the author and the story, and do not need "luring in" anew every episode via cliffhangers.

If you have made sure that your seasons, your long arc, and your short arcs are all working together to make the story irresistible to readers, then cliffhangers are not required for every single chapter or episode. They will happen organically when they should, but you will not need to *force* a cliffhanger on readers to keep them reading. You might get some fall off in numbers if a specific episode does not have a cliffhanger, but it's unlikely to be significant because most subscribers have committed to the long haul.

For them, it is less about a specific story's episode than the experience of being a fan of the author's work overall.

If you think I'm wrong, consider the way we read and write novels. No one is saying that *every* chapter in a novel *must* end on a cliffhanger in order to force the reader to keep going to the next chapter. They've already bought or borrowed the book, so at that point it needs to stand on its own and be interesting and well written, not contain a cliffhanger at the end of each chapter.

Yes, there are reasons why you might want to have cliffhangers at the end of every chapter of a novel. After all, whether you love his work or hate it, we all have to agree that this was a very profitable approach for Dan Brown. But there are many, *many* kinds of novels that don't have cliffhangers at the end of *each chapter* and people regularly read such novels all the way through.

I've stressed over and over in this book that serials are not novels, but in this case, they are pretty much the same: if you write a great story, then people will want to read it all the way through, cliffhangers or no.

If you are an author who is writing stories that don't lend themselves to multiple cliffhangers, or if you are simply an author who doesn't write that way, then a subscription model of your very own is a much better plan.

THREE

Serials in Practice

Online *serialized* stories are easy to find. You only need to look on platforms like AO3, Wattpad, Ream, RoyalRoad, and even Patreon to find them. The "Big 3" as of 2026 are:

- Ream is a newer platform that has been built from the ground up by authors, for authors, and while it only officially launched in May 2023, it gained traction fast. It is geared to the romance genre, and is an especially good choice for authors of any genre who write spicey/erotic fiction.
- Substack is a platform that has been around for a few years but is quickly becoming a new home for writers who are serializing stories across multiple genres, including those not usually seen on the other platforms like historical fiction, women's fiction, and literary fiction.

- Patreon is the "old standby" as it was one of the first platforms that authors could use to get paid directly by their readers. It remains popular despite its drawbacks for readers and authors alike, and some authors serialize stories on their own personal websites as well. If you are able to read Korean, Japanese, or Chinese, then you have a whole vista of online fiction platforms that really put the west to shame!

That said, not all the stories on those platforms are truly *serials*.

At this point, quite a few stories are *serialized versions of novels*. This is especially true in the romance genre, where many authors have done well by serializing their novels before publishing them as books. This is one reason my definition of a true *serial* story states that it has at least 100,000 words; chances are good that if you find a story well over that word count and/or it has fifty chapters and counting, then it is a serial.

This is why it is important to communicate with your readers about what you are really writing.

If they expect a novel but you shoot past that with no sign of stopping, they might get frustrated at what seems to be a story that will never end. Some readers could even accuse you of "dragging it out" for clicks/reads.

On the other hand, readers who are expecting a truly epic, layered, and long-lasting story but instead get taken out at the knees when the novel-sized story wraps up will be disappointed and confused.

All of this is to say, I went looking for text-based serials online and found a few, but it took a bit of research because, for instance, a lot of the top serialized original fiction (that is, *not* fanfiction) on various subscription platforms are actually novels.

RoyalRoad is an exception. Many fantasy, science fiction, and LitRPG stories that are valid, long-running serials are on the platform.

Earlier, I mentioned Substack, which is a "newsletter" platform that has been around for a few years but is now experiencing a renaissance in the wake of many authors abandoning other social media platforms. It's a cross between a social media platform and a newsletter publishing platform, so is rather unique, but if you just want to set up a paid newsletter without the social media bells and whistles for your serial, you can also use Ghost.io, Beehiiv, or my recommendation, Buttondown (not affiliated with them, I just like the founder and his principles).

A number of web serials have since been published as book series, so you can read those with an eye to duplicating the structure they used/are using:

- **Kazuma Kamachi:** *A Certain Magical Index* (19 volumes)
- **Drew Hayes:** Now publishes his serials exclusively as book series.
- **A.F. Kay:** Posts episodes of their serial *Divine Apostasy* first on Patreon, then publishes them as books.
- **Alexandra Erin:** Early adopter to online serials, whose original breakout *Tales of MU* began around 2010 and are now only available on Kindle Unlimited; the author continues to write serials on her Patreon.
- **Anna Todd:** Her *After* serial was a breakout hit on Wattpad and eventually sold to Simon & Schuster.

- **MXTX:** By both read and sales numbers, possibly the most popular author in the world; her works all started as long-running serials, including *Heaven Official's Blessing, Grandmaster of Demonic Cultivation,* and *Scum Villain's Self-Saving System.*
- **Priest:** All her works started as serials, including *Guardian, Sha Po Lang,* and *Mo Du.*

Of course, if you go looking for graphic stories/comics/manga, there are a plethora of options. From *One Piece* to *The Property of Hate* to the ongoing steampunk classic *Girl Genius* to the now-legendary *Lackadaisy* there are many to choose from. Some web comics I've followed on Mangatoons have been hundreds of chapters long (they are usually translations of existing, popular Chinese web comics).

I've talked about the *Chronicles of Narnia, Song of Fire and Ice, Lord of the Rings, Heaven Official's Blessing, Sha Po Lang,* and *Grand Master of Demonic Cultivation* as serials, even though the Western stories were published as novel series. One I did not mention, because I waffle back and forth on it, is the book series *Wheel of Time*; write me and let me know on which side of the coin you think it falls: serial or series of novels?

SERIAL VS. SERIES

Book Series to Serial

In the chapter <u>Serials are Different</u>, I noted that once you understand serials as a unique format, not just as a method of story delivery, you will look at a lot of trilogies and other book series you love differently.

Unfortunately, what is often the case is that a novel series is being treated as a serial, with books printed regularly for readers, but *without* the internal structure that makes long-lasting serials successful.

This becomes clear when the series fails.

We all know of a cozy mystery series that was really popular right up until the tenth or twentieth book. Suddenly, readers start complaining that all the murders are the same, there is no sizzling chemistry between the main character and their on-again, off-again romantic lead, and the town/village/suburb where the detective lives become less "cute" and more "dead end cul-de-sac."

I call this the "series void," where the repetition of the structure collapses into itself like a black hole. The story is stale, and readership falls off until the series stops being profitable and, worse, becomes *unenjoyable*.

What happened?

The author was treating the series like a collection of novels or an episodic television show. Usually, these are centered around what is called the "flat character arc," where the character has no significant character growth per se, but rather serves as a focal point for change (or murders) going on around them. How to Write a Series by Sara Rosett is a good resource on explaining exactly how that works and uses James Bond and Miss Marple as examples of this kind of story. (Her whole book is a great reference for series writing!)

Television shows featuring flat character arcs manage to go longer than novel series because of the visually stimulating nature of the medium, honestly. The reason *Columbo* (69 episodes) was so successful was because of the brilliance of Peter Falk's acting and presentation, not because the plots or settings were irresistible. Whereas Hercule Poirot has a canon of fifty stories, of which only thirty-three are novels, *Murder She Wrote* was 264 episodes long.

(Sitcoms go on *forever* because the actors and the comedy pull the audience in long after all the plot lines have jumped the shark. Reminder that *The Simpsons* are the exception to every rule.)

As authors, we might be able to lean on a mesmerizing lead character for a few books, but eventually, the interest wanes for both readers and authors. Even Arthur Conan Doyle and Agatha Christie grew to hate their most popular characters (Sherlock and Poirot, respectively).

Arthur Conan Doyle unintentionally dipped his toe into making the Sherlock Holmes series into a true serial by introducing Moriarty, but he pushed the stakes too high too soon (because he wanted to kill Sherlock off, but WE DON'T TALK ABOUT THAT IN THIS HOUSE).

But this shows what the secret sauce is to serials: *an ongoing, long arc*. That is what makes a serial different from a novel series.

You don't have to add a mastermind villain to your charming seaside bed-and-breakfast cozy mystery series, but you *do* need to add elements to the narrative beyond "quirky lead character" and "cleverly done murders." We got into details on how to do that in the Serial Beats section, but right now I want you to seriously consider: **what you really want to write?**

If you've decided to write (or are already writing) a novel series, consider how far out you want to take it. You might only have five or six (or three!) novels in you for that character/setup, and that's fine. You can write a series of connected novels as you originally intended.

But if you are hoping to keep the series going for five books or ten or twenty, you *need* to think of it as a serial instead. A serial will keep looping around to get readers reinvested in the narrative arc of the characters (even if she marries the love interest and all the murders look the same).

Serial to Book Series

The consideration you need to make going into writing a serial is whether, after online serialization, you intend to publish the story later in a different format. Usually, that means "some form of book," whether that is ebook and/or print, but can include audio as well. Serial authors who transfer their stories into discrete parts often create a *book series*. This has been done both more and less successfully over the years, and what you'll often find are "novel" series that are actually serials in format and structure, simply repackaged (or, in some instances, dismantled) into books.

I've already talked about examples like *The Chronicles of Narnia* and *The Lord of the Rings* (or, dare I say it, *Song of Ice and Fire*). There are a lot more out there.

As you start planning your serial, choose beat structures that give you natural break points for pulling out sections that can be turned into individual books. (I won't call them novels, since they are seasons or long arcs, depending how long they are and what you can stuff into a single book volume!).

The usual method of publishing a serial is by "arcs," which in practice are the serial's seasons, but it varies a lot because so many other factors come into play. Usually, books are created out of natural breaks in the story, such as the end of a season (arc), but sometimes publishers (or authors) will end a book on a cliffhanger to encourage new readers to buy the next book. If you use the *Unstoppable* beats method, you have built-in breaks in the form of "seasons" that are good for partitioning out as individual books. Knowing this, you can plan out your future book publishing goals and time them to your serial posts.

Another important consideration is whether you want to pull the online serial version down in order to publish it. If you get a deal with a traditional publisher, you might not have a choice; the contract may require you to take it down so it is not available elsewhere. If that idea bothers you, then fight for the right to keep the story "live" online in any publishing contracts.

There are lots of ways to "deliver" your story, though. One example is that you could publish a book of the first season while already posting episodes of season two. At that point, existing fans would want to buy the first season as a collectible, so consider doing special editions (digital and print) only available on your online store. Then have less-fancy versions for sale on all the usual book distributor sites ('zon, B&N, Kobo, etc.) at a later date, possibly with a traditional book marketing campaign, to draw new readers in. Make sure your book's back matter informs the reader that season two is already ongoing, with a call to action for them to sign up to read it via your subscription platform/newsletter.

That is just one way to build up to and optimize creating a book series out of your serial. For more suggestions and advice from authors already doing this, check out the facebook group Subscriptions for Authors.

ONLINE SERIALS

Here are a few online serials which are worth exploring, not just as research material but because they are fun to read. I am sure there are more out there than I know about or have managed to find, so please feel free to recommend one to me!

- Worm by John C. McCrae (Wildbow), approx. 1.5 million words.
- The Wandering Inn by Pirateaba, 11 million words (yes, really) and ongoing.
- Worth the Candle by Alexander Wales, 1.7 million words.
- Mother of Learning by Domagoi Kumaic (nobody103), 800k words (the top-rated story on RoyalRoad, years running.)
- Reborn as a Demonic Tree by Xkarnation is a newer serial but already tremendously popular. It's only 200k words long at this point, but they only started posting at the start of 2023, and update five times a week.
- Tales from the Triverse by Simon K. Jones, a trailblazer on Substack who started posting serial fiction there back in 2021. This serial is now complete and clocks in at over 400,000 words.
- Underline the Rainbow by Not-Poignant on AO3 (although it is original fiction, not fanfic). A massively prolific serial fiction author, Not-Poignant writes serials that often run to hundreds of thousands of words. This is part of their massive, sprawling "Fae Tales" which have an absolutely dedicated, loyal following. (Please do mind the tags, though, these stories are not for everyone!)
- Fanfiction: There are a lot of serials in fanfiction, and many run between 200k and 1 million+ words long. While fanfiction may not be your "thing," it might be worth your time to go to AO3, find a fandom you are familiar with or is popular (*Star Wars, Star Trek, Minecraft,*

Supernatural, etc.) and do a search for both the longest and the most popular story in that fandom to study what the writers have done. *However*, please be respectful of the fact that most fanfiction writers are not professional authors and that you are visiting a "hobbyist space" with its own culture. Be respectful, be polite!

SUBSCRIPTION PLATFORMS FOR SERIALS

While it is entirely possible for you to print out episodes of your serial and mail them in envelopes to your followers (David Viergutz uses this model for his "scaremail" horror fiction subscription, and makes a lot of money doing it), we have the advantage of living in an Internet-driven world and can easily post our stories on line.

There are a lot of platforms these days that are good for doing that, and over the past ten years we have seen an explosion of options for authors to use. Some are very new, and some "old" (by Internet standards). When I first started thinking about serializing stories online, pickings were slim and not very reader friendly (or author friendly, for that matter). I actually considered rolling my own website using WordPress and assorted plugins, but that felt overwhelming.

Below is a list of current, popular platforms for posting your work. Some pay directly, some offer subscriptions, and some are not monetized at all. You have to consider who your demographic is among a lot of other factors to decide which one is right for you. Some authors only publish on Ream, others only on Vella, and some post on multiple platforms (you have to be careful about terms of service in that case, since some platforms do not want work shared anywhere else).

Some platforms allow you to charge "membership" subscriptions for readers, while others are "free to post and read." The latter often serves as a funnel to the former, so think carefully about where your story fits genre-wise and the kind of subscription model you want to set up.

Here's the brief list, with links (if you are reading the print version, these links are on the resources webpage provided at the start of the book):

- Ream
- Substack
- Patreon
- RoyalRoad
- Inkitt/Galatea
- Wattpad
- Scribble Hub
- Tapas
- Webnovel

So, what happened to Vella and Radish and so many other platforms that used to be popular? They closed down, victims in my opinion of both greed and technological progress.

Those platforms functioned a lot like Kindle Unlimited or Spotify: you pay the platform for unlimited access to a bunch of stuff. In turn, the platform turns around and pays out a pittance to the creator who did all the work. While some authors did manage to make a few large paychecks on those sites, they were always susceptible to the algorithm and the greed of the platform owners.

The reason those platforms appeared in the first place was that for a long time, setting up a payment system to take a reader's money was just plain *difficult*. Payment gateways, merchant services, and back-end website development took time, money, and expertise. Most authors were too busy writing!

But technology caught up, and now any author with a basic understanding of WordPress or Squarespace can set up a direct sales shop and charge for membership. Sites like Patreon, Ream, and Substack make it even easier, while adding the benefit of creating a good "reading space" for fiction works.

I think we are living in a time of unique and nearly unlimited opportunity for serials and serialization! Sure, the same old challenges remain: We have to write the stories, get them edited, create cover art, publish them, promote them, advertise them…none of that ever changes. But the new creator economy is just now starting to lift off, and I am excited to be here for it!

Afterward (2023)

To be perfectly honest, the reason I wrote this book is that I love serial stories and want more of them in the world!

This love of serials started early for me with *The Black Stallion*, which I became obsessed with as a girl. I read the book series all the way through until my reading level outgrew it and I moved on to stories like *Dune* and *Watership Down*. Yet I've never forgotten the thrill of getting *the next book* in the series, reading it, and then moving on to the *next one*. I know a lot of my peers were similarly entranced with Nancy Drew or the Hardy Boys, and of course there was Anne of Green Gables. Book series have been a staple of preadolescent reading for about 200 years at this point, and those of us who read a lot as children can quickly tell you *everything* about the series we grew up with.

Then we grow up. Oh, the tragedy!

But I kept looking for stories that *kept going*, reading a lot of fantasy and science fiction trilogies and series. I owned a copy of the *Dune Encyclopedia* so I could reference it as I read. I never got into *Lord of the Rings*, for reasons that mystify me at this point, as I'm pretty sure I would have loved it (I sure do love the movies!). Predictably, I became a huge fan of the *Star Wars* and *Star Trek* franchises, for reasons which should be clear at this point!

So, for me, it represents the closing of a circle to return to *ongoing stories* as a writer. When I first shared The Spreadsheet, I was not expecting very many people to care about it, but many authors jumped in with both feet and wanted more! Which, of course, led to this book.

I hope it has helped you to decide if you want to write a serial and provided guidance on how to do it. I am a very intuitive discovery writer, and writing all of this out was a way for me to understand what I was doing instinctively.

My own goal is to invest myself into the serial stories I want to tell, no holds barred! No more will I try to shoehorn myself into a story form that does not fit me as an author. I'm very excited about the brave new world of serials, which I fully expect to become massive over the next few years.

See ya' there!

Afterward (2026)

It's hard to believe what this little book has done for me and for a lot of authors I know in just three years!

As I mentioned earlier, this whole thing started as a barely-there spreadsheet and a facebook post. Then came webinars, writing this book, multiple podcast appearances, and eventually a chance to present on the topic of serials at AuthorNation 2025!

All that said, I was highly resistant to doing anything more than that. Friends kept telling me to start a community, teach courses, do *something*. But honestly, having written the book and talked about it for two+ years, I figured there wasn't much more I could do.

Then, after my presentation at AuthorNation 2025, *several* people came up to me and told me that I should do webinars, seminars, and courses on the topic. They said there was a need in the community, and my approach had something special to offer writers who wanted to start serializing.

I demured. What more did I have to say, anyway? Nothing helpful, I was sure!

But the universe has a way of beating you about the head with something it doesn't want you to ignore, and eventually, I finally realized something was far more important than my hesitation and doubts: We are living through an unprecedented time.

It feels like the early days of widespread internet adaptation in the '90s. It feels like the breaking of the dam in 2008 when "ebooks" became a talking point (mostly due to the release of the first Kindle device in late 2007). Nowadays, it's all about artificial intelligence.

I'm not here to convince you to love it or hate it; it is what it is, and despite the fondest hopes of some people, it is here to stay. It's early days for this technology, yet it is already shifting the ground under our feet.

So what does that mean for authors? More importantly, what does that mean for *storytellers*? After all, I know a lot of authors who are extremely business focused and are already pumping out books using A.I. assistance. They are doing so successfully, and chances are, you've read one of their books and not even realized it. I can't sugar coat that for you.

Yet, I truly believe we are in a time of renaissance for storytellers. People who, like me, are "in it for the game." We love developing and writing the stories in our heads and hearts, and no robot is going to change that.

(One of my favorite online artists recently posted a lovely rumination on this which I highly recommend!)

In the midst of all this, I have looked around and decided that serialization (of serials, novels, or non-fiction) can become a vital connection between storytellers and readers. It is a great time to connect with people who love exactly what you love and want to immerse themselves in your work over long stretches of time. Now more than ever, readers are looking for ways to *enjoy* reading again, instead of it feeling like an obligation they don't have time for.

And so, thanks to those insights (as well as repeated interventions by friends who *insisted* that I need to do this!) I've launched Serial Nation Academy. It's not just resources, it's a way to connect with my explorations and insights on what is happening in the land of serials online. I'd love to see you there! I've got a lot in store!

Thanks for reading this far, and I hope to see you around, either online or in person! Please drop by and say hi!

Join the Serial Nation!

Now that you have the blueprints, it's time to get your hands dirty—but you don't have to build this engine alone in the dark! Serial Nation is the home base for authors exploring this new (old!) way to write and publish. I host webinars, share helpful resources, host regular "launch pad" cohorts, and build a community of writers helping writers! Whether you need deep-dive tactics, a supportive crew for the long haul, or just a fresh pot of coffee, I've got a seat saved for you!

$\int$erial
Nation

KimBoo York

AUTHOR + FANGIRL

KimBoo York is a GenX fangirl who is also a librarian, former project manager, and a professional author who enjoys talking to other authors about productivity, data management, serialization, and, yes, fanfiction! She has been told that her writing crosses too many genres, including romance, fantasy, and non-fiction, but she keeps doing it anyway. She lives on coffee and hope!

She/her/hers | Cis | Bisexual | Jewish | Crone | Intersectional Feminist | Anti-Colonialist | Socialist | BLM | Anti-TERF | Antifa | Anti-MAGA!

Get more advice on writing publishing serials at www.serial-nation.com!

Full Copyright